MYSTERIOUS PLACES

Also by Daniel Cohen

MYTHS OF THE SPACE AGE

SECRETS FROM ANCIENT GRAVES

MYSTERIOUS PLACES

DANIEL COHEN

ILLUSTRATED

DODD, MEAD *&* COMPANY

NEW YORK

Library of Congress Catalog Card Number: 77-75787
Printed in the United States of America
by The Cornwall Press, Inc., Cornwall, N. Y.

To my father,
who has as much love of the future
as I have of the past

INTRODUCTION

Imagine an archaeological team in the seventieth century A.D. excavating the site of an ancient city and coming upon the ruins of Disneyland. What would they make of it?

If future archaeologists are at all like current ones they might well decide it was a temple complex or a cult center established for the worship of a mouse-god and subordinate animal deities.

Or imagine a seventieth-century scholar examining the fragmentary remains of twentieth-century documents and picking up scattered references to The Land of Oz. Would he have reason to believe that Oz was not a real place? He might even develop an elaborate theory concerning the catastrophe that destroyed Oz, to account for the lack of physical evidence for the place.

Disneyland and Oz might be included in a seventieth-century version of this book, for this is a book about puzzling places, real, unreal and uncertain. I have embarked, quite frankly, on an excursion into romantic geography, for all the places discussed in the pages that follow have somehow captured men's imaginations and caused them to weave legends.

My aims are twofold. First, of course, is to give the facts, to show what historical realities underlie the legends. But equally important I want to relate the legends themselves.

Often the legend was more real than the place. King Arthur's realm, if it existed at all, was of minor importance, and the kingdom of Prester John was entirely legendary. Yet both these lands had a tremendous impact on the thinking of medieval Europe.

It's really not surprising that the medieval European, who knew almost nothing of Asia, should believe that the Mongol conqueror Genghis Khan ruled a mighty Christian empire. It is somewhat more surprising to realize that many twentieth-century Americans believe that the cities of South America, the statues of Easter Island and a stone city in the middle of Africa were built by white men. But the fact that such ideas continually crop up, speaks volumes about our own state of mind.

In researching this book I was continually astounded at the number of times I came across legends of white gods, white culture bearers, vanished civilizations of white men, etc., and how little basis there was to any of these stories.

I have tried to give equal exposure to the reasonable specula-tions of scholars and to the incredible ideas of cranks, for the cranks have often been more influential in shaping public thinking than the scholars. I'm sure that more people have heard of Atlantis because it is mentioned prominently in the prophecies of modern occultists, than because archaeologists believe they have found a real basis for the story.

Then there is the problem of deciding just who holds the crank theory anyway. Gerald Hawkins, the astronomer who proposed that Stonehenge was used as an astronomical observ-atory and computer is widely believed to have "solved" the mystery of Stonehenge. The popular opinion is not shared by archaeologists who have spent years studying the monument. Not that the scholars consider Hawkins' theories as crankish—not quite. But they have been called "tendentious, arrogant, slipshod and unconvincing."

Reasonable and unreasonable, sound and foolish, they all should have their say because they are all part of the story. The mystery itself, and how it grew, is as important and interesting as the solution.

My basic reason for selecting these particular ten places is that they have interested me. From an information standpoint they are a mixed lot. Both Atlantis and Stonehenge have received a great deal of publicity. In addition to tons of nonsense that has been written on both places they have also been the subject of a number of excellent popular treatments. However, in both cases there have been some remarkable discoveries, or at least theories in the past few years that justify a reexamination.

Other places, like the kingdom of Prester John, and Lemuria, have received surprisingly little popular attention. They are merely referred to as legendary, with no hint of how and why the legends began.

Basically this is a book to be read for fun. It is for people who are fascinated by exotic places and ancient mysteries. Let's face it, whether Atlantis existed or not has very little relevance in our everyday life. If this book is to "teach" anything I suppose it is the need for intellectual humility and caution. After reviewing all the wonderful theories of the past, and seeing how embarrassingly wide of the mark most of them have been, one realizes that many of the reasonable theories of today may turn out to be equally wrong.

Most suspect of all are those grand theories which presume

to explain all questions in a single sweep. There are enough uncertainties to allow the known facts to be squeezed and pushed into some sort of relationship with one another. A grand all-encompassing answer is the most satisfying explanation, but it is not necessarily the correct one.

I have as much passion for the nice, well-constructed solution as the next man—but I have had to leave many questions unanswered, and many clues without conclusions. It is in the nature of the subject. Even the conclusions presented are tentative. I found myself often using words like probably, perhaps and apparently. When handling this sort of material an author lives in perpetual terror that between the time the manuscript is delivered to the publisher and the time the finished book reaches the reader some startling and totally unexpected discovery will be announced, and a pet conclusion that had been carefully nurtured and lovingly presented will be shattered beyond repair.

A word must be added about the spelling of proper names, because if they are translations, particularly translations from ancient languages, they vary according to the authority consulted. Take the name Genghis Kahn; it is also commonly spelled Gengis, Jenghiz, Jenghis, Chinghiz or Chingiz. I consulted an authoritative biography of the Mongol conqueror in which the translator insisted that the correct English form was Chingis, and deplored all other forms of spelling. After all that the fellow's book was filed in the New York Public Library under Genghis Khan. I make no pretense at presenting a scholarly treatise, and I have chosen those spellings which I believe will be most familiar to a general readership.

Enough explanations—it's time to venture into the lands of the lost. I hope you find the journey enlightening and most of all entertaining.

CONTENTS

xi

CONTENTS

ILLUSTRATIONS

ILLUSTRATIONS

MYSTERIOUS PLACES

ATLANTIS

Everybody's Paradise Lost

One gets the impression that if Plato had been just a bit less garrulous, the story of Atlantis, and the millions upon millions of words that have been written about it, would not exist. Throughout history the legions who have searched for the lost continent have agreed on only one thing—it all started with Plato.

But I suspect that if Plato had never mentioned Atlantis, someone else would have; for in one sense Atlantis is just the gaudiest and most persistent embodiment of that overpowering human belief that somewhere, a long time ago, life was much better than it is today—but that the place was destroyed, and the golden age lost. The idea of evolution, both biological and cultural, is a fairly new one. The concept of the Fall is much older and more widely accepted. Man seems to get some obscure but great satisfaction from feeling that the world is bad and getting worse.

There are really two roads to Atlantis. The first leads to the land of the imagination. It has been well traveled, and widely advertised, so much so that it has almost discouraged people from seeking the second road which quite possibly leads to a real place of stone and soil, inhabited by real people, that really was destroyed in an awesome catastrophe.

Both roads begin in Athens.

About 355 B.C. when Plato was over seventy years of age he planned to write a trilogy, in which the story of Atlantis figured importantly. The first part was called *Timaios*, and contains an account of the creation of the world and the nature of man; it also contains Plato's most complete account of Atlantis. The second part, *Kritias*, was to go into the story of Atlantis in more detail, but Plato abandoned the project in the middle. The third part, *Hermokrates*, was never even begun. Instead Plato went on to write *The Laws* and died before returning to what might be called his Atlantean trilogy.

Plato laid out his ideas in playlets called dialogues. A group of prominent people, invariably led by Plato's famous old teacher Socrates, sit around and discuss various philosophical and moral questions. The discussion about Atlantis was to have taken place about 421 B.C.

The characters in these playlets are real enough. Socrates is certainly well known. Kritias was a distant relative of Plato himself, and one of these particularly enigmatic Greek figures, poet, scholar and scoundrel. Timaios was an astronomer from Italy and Hermokrates was a general from Syracuse, living in exile in Athens.

The four met at Kritias' house early in June. On the previous day the same four men had been discussing the ideal government, a discussion which had resulted in Plato's most famous dialogue, *The Republic*.

Did these four men ever really have such a discussion?

Probably not, and if they had, Plato could not have recorded it accurately for in 421 he was a small child. It is safe enough to assume that Plato is simply putting his own ideas into the mouths of other men.

Timaios was supposed to speak first on the "Principals of Cosmology and Physical Science." But Hermokrates interrupts and mentions "a story derived from ancient tradition" that Kritias knows. Kritias is pressed to repeat it, and so begins the tale of Atlantis.

The story had been in Kritias' family for generations. His ancestors heard it a century and a half before from the great Athenian statesman Solon, who had heard it in Egypt. Solon was a real person, and he did make a trip to Egypt, although there is some discrepancy between the time he actually made his Egyptian journey and the time Plato has him making it.

In Plato's story, Solon stopped at the Egyptian city of Sais, where he fell into a discussion of ancient history with some Egyptian priests. Solon tried to impress the priests by telling them of the antiquity of some Greek traditions. But the Egyptians just laughed, and told him the Greeks were like children and knew nothing of ancient history because all their records had been destroyed in periodic catastrophes, which engulf the world. All the world but Egypt that is, because said the oldest priest, Egypt preserved all the records that had been made from the time of the creation of the world on down.

But rather than boasting of the antiquity of Egypt, the priest flattered Athens and told Solon that the goddess Athena had founded a great Athenian empire some nine thousand years previously, or by our reckoning 9600 B.C. At the same time there had been a second great empire, that of Atlantis, which was located on an enormous island to the west of the Pillars of Hercules (our Strait of Gibraltar). The island continent of Atlantis was as big as North Africa and Asia Minor combined.

While the ancient Athenians were "the fairest and noblest race of men that ever lived," the Atlanteans had become decadent and greedy. They tried to conquer the cities of the Mediterranean region, including Athens. But the Athenians alone stood against them, defeating them in battle after battle. "But just then there happened exceedingly violent earthquakes and great floods," said the priest. "In one terrible day and night all of your warriors in a body were swallowed up . . . and in a like manner the Island of Atlantis sank into the sea, and vanished. Even now the ocean at its former location cannot be crossed or explored as there is a great shoal of mud in the way, a consequence of the foundering of the island."

So Kritias finished his tale. Socrates was delighted, saying that "the fact that it was not an invented tale but authentic history was of the greatest importance." The philosopher and his friends decided to allow Kritias to expand on the subject of Atlantis on the following day when they were scheduled to discuss the behavior of citizens of a well-ordered state during a national emergency.

The next day Kritias takes up the story. He begins by describing the golden age which existed when both Athens and Atlantis were founded nine thousand years ago. There is an inconsistency here, for on the previous day he had both nations being destroyed nine thousand years ago, and this was supposed to be "many generations" after their founding.

Atlantis had been given to the sea god Poseidon, and the god populated it mainly with his own descendants by the mortal maid Kleito. The land was divided among his ten sons, who ruled as a confederacy of kings. The eldest, Atlas (after whom Atlantis was named), was made chief king.

4

The kings and their descendants built the city of Atlantis on the southern coast of their island continent. It was a circular city, regular in dimensions. In the center of the city was the hill which contained the original dwelling place of Poseidon and Kleito. This had been converted into a temple surrounded by a golden wall. Around the hill were two rings of land and three of water, which made up a circular citadel three miles in diameter. The entire metropolis was about fifteen miles in diameter. A great ship canal ran from the sea, through the center of the city and to an irrigated plain beyond it. This plain was rectangular in shape, and divided into regular square lots which were assigned to farmers, who in turn had to furnish men for the Atlantean army.

The kings met together every few years and, after sacrificing a sacred bull with great ceremony, spent a day and a night conducting the business of governing their land and dispensing its laws.

For generations the Atlanteans lived virtuously amid their wealth, but eventually greed got the better of them. Zeus, king of the gods, decided they had to be punished. He called together all his fellow gods to discuss what should be done ". . . and when he had assembled them, he spake thus: . . ."

And that's just where Plato decided to drop the story. The destruction of Atlantis, the detail of the story that has so fascinated later times, is only described in the barest outline.

What do we have in this incomplete story: sober history, an imperfectly remembered tradition of some catastrophe or pure myth? All three explanations have been put forward with great force and at great length throughout the centuries.

There is no mention of the existence of Atlantis in any Greek literature before Plato. True, not that much pre-Platonic Greek literature survives, and Plato seems to indicate that the Atlantis story was one that was kept in his own family (remember Kritias was Plato's kinsman) and not widely known. But the lack of other references is disquieting. Even more disturbing is that there is no mention of Atlantis in any literature from any ancient civilization, including the Egyptians, from whom Solon was supposed to have received the information in the first place. Fairly extensive ancient Egyptian records have survived. The literature of most ancient civilizations contains stories of the cataclysmic destruction of great areas of land, but none of these can be clearly related to the cataclysm that was supposed to have resulted in the sinking of Atlantis.

Most disturbing of all, however, is that we can find no archaeological evidence to support the literal truth of Plato's story. How, you might wonder, are we to find the ruins of Atlantis, when Atlantis has sunk to the bottom of the sea? But such an objection does not take into account the Atlanteans' great foe, the ancient Athenians. Now these Athenians of 9600 B.C. were more important to Plato than the Atlanteans, for the few who survived the catastrophe (remember Athens as well as Atlantis was destroyed, but only the land of Atlantis sank) became the Athenians of his own day. Greece has been well explored archaeologically, and not a trace of this really ancient Athenian civilization has been found. The argument that all traces were destroyed in the catastrophe does not hold, because from an archaeological point of view natural catastrophes are a boon. The best-preserved archaeological sites in the world are Pompeii and Herculaneum, Roman cities overwhelmed in a volcanic eruption.

From everything we know about the development of human civilization, there is something wrong with this 9600 B.C. date.

The oldest civilizations we know of date back only to the fourth millennium B.C. Perhaps future discoveries will push this date back somewhat, but not five thousand years. During the ninth millennium B.C. man lived under extremely primitive conditions; there is not the slightest hint that an advanced civilization existed anywhere.

From all available evidence, those scholars who followed Plato regarded his Atlantis story as a fable. Plato's most famous pupil Aristotle collected facts covering almost every aspect of human knowledge, yet he mentions Atlantis only once, and his comment is ironic: "He who invented it also destroyed it."

A few centuries later the philosopher Poseidonios thought that, considering all that was known about earthquakes, erosion and other forces that destroyed land, "it is possible that the story about the island of Atlantis is not a fiction." Still later the Roman scholar Pliny the Elder prefaces a remark about Atlantis with the phrase "if we are to believe Plato." When Plutarch, a contemporary of Pliny's, wrote his biography of Solon he mentioned the statesman's desire to write a poem of "the history or fable of the Atlantic Island."

We have now carried the opinions about Atlantis well into the era of the Roman Empire, and the value of evidence and logic which the Greeks had introduced is fast disappearing. This era saw the growth of the Neoplatonists, a semimystical, semiphilosophical cult that used the writings of Plato as a springboard into wilder flights of fancy. It was the Neoplatonists who first began to treat the story of Atlantis in dead earnest. Lacking any new evidence to bolster Plato's questionable tale, the Neoplatonists began to invent evidence. Plotinos, one of the Neoplatonists, found Egyptian columns inscribed with the tale of Atlantis. Unfortunately no one else ever found them.

As Christianity spread throughout the Roman Empire, interest in Atlantis waned. The last significant mention of Atlantis for many centuries appears in a work written by Kosmas, a sixth-century Egyptian monk. Kosmas has earned himself a small but secure niche in the history of error. In his *Christian Topography* Kosmas tried to show that the pagan Greeks had been wrong when they said the world was round. According to the monk, the world was flat, as the ancient Hebrews had believed. Atlantis, Kosmas said, was nothing more than a garbled version of the Biblical flood story.

When the age of exploration dawned in the fifteenth century, cartographers dotted their maps of the Atlantic with a host of large nonexistent islands. Whether these islands were purely imaginary or had some basis in imperfectly recalled accounts of actual Atlantic exploration (perhaps by the Phoenicians, or by the Vikings who did for a time colonize the New World about A.D. 1000), it is hard to determine. But the idea that there was some new land to the west was current in Europe. Christopher Columbus believed none of this. He was a follower of the ancient geographer Ptolemy, who held that the land surface of the earth was far greater than the water surface. Columbus was not looking for new lands when he set sail. He expected to reach the Asian mainland, and was both surprised and chagrined when he found there was unexpected land in his way. Columbus carried letters from the monarch of Spain to the Great Kahn of Cathay, and he sailed around the Caribbean asking the natives to lead him to the palace of the Kahn. Only slowly and reluctantly did it dawn upon him that the islands he discovered were not just off the mainland of Asia.

Columbus' discovery brought Atlantis to the surface once again. America, many reasoned, must be Atlantis, or at least Plato had heard rumors of America and this had given him the kernal of truth for his Atlantis story. Some elaborated the theory in this way: America had been part of Atlantis, but after the catastrophe the part of Atlantis nearer Europe sank and the sea became unnavigable. This deprived Europe of all certain knowledge of the Atlantic continent. As late as the eighteenth century some stubborn cartographers insisted on calling America Atlantis on their maps. The whole Atlantis-in-America theory gained a small but fairly respectable following, including Sir Francis Bacon, the naturalist Buffon and the great German explorer Alexander von Humboldt. But the more Europeans learned about America the less it seemed to resemble Plato's Atlantis, and the whole theory was ultimately abandoned.

To some Europeans, the discovery of America presented difficulties of another sort. From ancient times there had been plenty of tales of distant lands inhabited by monstrous semi-human creatures. So if the inhabitants of America had arms like snakes, or faces in the middle of their chests, this would merely have confirmed ancient wisdom. Most Europeans were even prepared to accept the idea of naked savages, and there were plenty of people in the Americas who could be placed in that pigeonhole. Opinion varied as to whether the American Indians were "noble savages" living in some sort of exalted "state of nature" or a separate species of mankind created by the devil. The second idea was preferred since it provided a perfect excuse to massacre and exploit the Indians. What Europeans were unprepared for, however, was the discovery of civilized peoples. The Aztecs, Maya and Incas had flourishing cultures. These had apparently developed without the assistance and without even the knowledge of white men from Europe. It was not natural, it was not neat, and somehow it had to be accounted for.

Many attempts were made to incorporate the American Indians into Western history. For a time it was believed they were descendants of the Ten Lost Tribes of Israel. Others believed the Indians were Egyptians, Phoenicians, Assyrians, Scandinavians, Chinese and Lord knows what else. But slowly the idea that the American Indians were refugees from the catastrophe that destroyed Atlantis began to take root.

Those who find the Atlanteans in America cite as proof translations of Indian documents describing the sinking of the motherland and the flight to a new world. Virtually all these translations stem from the work of Diego de Landa, Bishop of Yucatán in the days following the Spanish conquest of Mexico. Of all the American Indians, only the Mayans, as far as we know, had a considerable written literature. De Landa, as spiritual overseer of the Maya area, was blind to the treasures he might have preserved. "We found a large number of books in these characters [Mayan hieroglyphics] and, as they contained nothing in which there were not to be seen superstition and lies of the devil, we burned them all, which they [the Maya] regretted to an amazing degree, and which caused them much affliction." Scholars have been condemning the bishop to the fires of hell ever since, yet he played a strange part in preserving the bits of Maya literature he left unburnt. De Landa compiled what he thought to be a translation of the Mayan alphabet into Spanish. Unfortunately he misunderstood the nature of the Mayan language, and his famous "alphabet" has led to much confusion, but it is about all we have, and it remains a vital tool in the continuing attempt to translate the Maya hieroglyphics.

De Landa was convinced the Maya were really the Ten Lost Tribes of Israel. In light of the knowledge and prejudices of the day this was a perfectly acceptable, even orthodox Christian idea. Then in 1864 a highly unorthodox Christian scholar, the Abbé Charles-Étienne Brasseur de Bourbourg, unearthed an abridged copy of de Landa's forgotten Mayan "dictionary." Brasseur was already much interested in America and the origins of the Indians. He had traveled widely in the New World, making some genuine historical and archaeological contributions. But armed with de Landa's incorrect alphabet, Brasseur made his most questionable contribution to the history of the American Indians. He translated one of the surviving Maya documents called the Troanto Codex (codex means book or manuscript). His translation contained a disorderly, often incoherent description of a great catastrophe. Brasseur even invented a name for the land destroyed in the catastrophe. It was called Mu, because two symbols which Brassuer could not otherwise account for seemed to resemble the M and U in de Landa's alphabet. The story of the catastrophe was too tantalizingly close to Plato's tale of the sinking of Atlantis. Brasseur noted similarities between the story of Atlantis and other Central American legends, but he made no attempt to develop the idea any further.

Brasseur's translations of the Mayan writings are sheer nonsense and were recognized as such even in his own day. But they have been used as one of the pillars of the edifice of Atlantis "scholarship."

The study of Atlantis remained a mere collection of odd facts and unmade connections until 1882, when Ignatius T. Donnelly came along and tied up all the loose ends, at least to his own satisfaction. Donnelly is a remarkable and strangely attractive character. He was a man of enormous intellectual and physical energy. At twenty-eight he was elected Lieutenant-Governor of Minnesota. Later he served two terms in Congress, and after being defeated ran for vice-president on the Populist Party ticket, a party he had helped start. He found time amid his many political activities to do a staggering amount of reading to support several curious ideas that he had developed, particularly ideas about Atlantis.

Donnelly's book *Atlantis: The Antediluvian World* has become the bible of modern Atlantism. Although it was published well over three quarters of a century ago, it is still widely available today.

In brief, Donnelly believed that Atlantis not only existed but that it was the original homeland of all civilizations, from the Egyptians to the Mayans. He also held that all memories of a lost Golden Age, the Garden of Eden, the Gardens of the Hesperides, the Elysian Fields, Olympus, Asgard and the rest are a "universal memory of a great land where early mankind dwelt for ages in peace and happiness."

After the disaster, says Donnelly, a few survivors fled to the lands east and west, bringing with them "tidings of the appalling catastrophe, which has survived in our own time in the Flood and Deluge legends of the different nations of the old and new world." Christian theorists saw the Atlantis legend as a distortion of the Biblical flood story; the Altantists have a cavalier attitude toward the Bible and see the story the other way round.

At about the same time Donnelly was writing, a French physician, Augustus Le Plongeon, was coming to approximately the same conclusions while digging around the Mayan ruins in Yucatán. Le Plongeon was much impressed by Brasseur's enthusiastically incorrect translations and carried them even further. One of Le Plongeon's favorite techniques was to identify a decorative part of a Mayan work of art as hieroglyphics and then translate it. No one else could make head or tail of his methods, but this did not deter Le Plongeon from denouncing all other scholars as a pack of fools and liars. He also began dragging in the works of occultists to support his own astounding conclusions. The study of Atlantis, which had started at a pretty low level, was declining fast.

In 1912 *The New York American* printed an article with what may well be one of the most egocentric titles ever devised, "How I Discovered Atlantis, the Source of All Civilization." The writer was Paul Schliemann, grandson of the fabulous German archaeologist Heinrich Schliemann. The younger Schliemann said that his famous grandfather had left him a large number of documents and artifacts which proved the existence of Atlantis. He stole shamelessly from Donnelly and Le Plongeon, without crediting his sources. If Donnelly and Le Plongeon were cranks, at least they were honest. Schliemann was a complete faker, and when pressed to present those marvelous artifacts to public view, he first hesitated, and then fell silent. The game was up. Or was it? One can still find Schliemann quoted with approval in the works of current Atlantists, who often confuse him with his grandfather.

One of the most unpleasant branches of Atlantist "scholarship" burst into flower with the rise of the Nazis in Germany. Several Nazi-influenced scholars tried to prove that Atlantis had been the original homeland of the superior Aryan race. They even went so far as to remove Plato's island continent from the middle of the Atlantic Ocean to the North Sea in order to get it closer to the Fatherland. In the 1930s there appeared in Germany a book called *Atlantis-Helgoland, Motherland of Aryan-Germanic Racial Thoroughbreeding and*

Colonization. As late as 1952, one German historian spent time chugging about the North Sea in a small motorboat looking for sunken cities. He was convinced that he had found Atlantis, but he could not generate much popular enthusiasm for his discovery.

It would be unfair to conclude, however, that all of those who have believed in the literal truth of Plato's story have been so foolish or so evil as the examples cited so far. The Scottish mythologist Lewis Spence was interested in the subject from the 1920s to the 1940s. At first he was quite skeptical; ". . . definite proof is conspicuous by its absence," he wrote. Later, proof became less necessary. The theories he developed were moderate enough in a field where excess is the rule. According to Spence the great continent had not disappeared in a single disaster but had sunk slowly over hundreds of years. He did not see the people of Atlantis as representatives of lost supercivilization but as possessors of a superior stone age culture.

In his later years Spence seemed to despair that the archaeology of his day would ever produce the needed proof for Atlantis. He spoke a bit wistfully perhaps of "inspirational methods" that would become "the Archaeology of the Future. The Tape-Measure School, dull and full of the credulity of incredulity, is doomed." He explained, "The day is passing when mere weight of evidence alone, unsupported by considerations which result from inspiration or insight, can be accepted by the world . . ."

Inspiration and insight have their place in archaeology, as they do in every other science, but the weight of evidence is still of paramount importance. Those whom Spence denounced as "the Tape-Measure School" carried the day among the professionals, and Spence's theories gathered no support from that quarter. On the other hand, he never found much favor among the occultists either.

Spence's reward for his moderation has been obscurity. Basically the poor fellow was just too tame for the occultists, who have, over the past century, sought to make Atlantis their very own. Antlantiology was squarely placed into the mystical cult of Theosophy by its founder, Madame Helena P. Blavatsky, who quarried Donnelly's book for most of her Atlantis "inspirations."

Today no mystic worth his salt can go through his career without some reference to the sinking and reemergence of Atlantis. A current favorite is Edgar Cayce, a mystic healer and prophet who died in 1945 but whose cult experienced a revival in the late 1960s. One of Cayce's pet prophecies was that Atlantis would rise again by the end of the decade of the 1960s and that this would be the first signal of a series of world-wide geological catastrophes, which include the abrupt sinking of California, New York and Japan.

Indeed the idea that Atlantis will rise again has become so firmly embedded in public consciousness that several years ago when a group of British newspapermen were asked to list the most important story they could imagine, they placed the reemergence of Atlantis fourth. It rated five places ahead of the Second Coming of Christ.

It is proper at this point to ask not only could Atlantis rise again, but could any land mass of that size have ever sunk within the time that man has existed on earth. Those who believe in Atlantis have always been weak on formulating a theory to account for the sinking of a continent, either in a single day and night or over a period of years. Of course they have tried. Some have postulated great gas-filled caverns under the earth which collapsed, submerging the land. Others, notably Hans Horbiger, have postulated the capture and destruction of various moons as providing the force for the catastrophe. One said Atlantis sank when it was struck by a giant comet, and in recent years Immanuel Velikovsky said the catastrophe was caused by the close approach of a giant comet.

In light of the geological knowledge of today, we must conclude that the sinking of a great middle Atlantic island, without leaving a trace, is highly improbable. At one time, when we knew a good deal less about the forces that shape the earth than we do today, it was permissible to postulate all sorts of trans-Atlantic land bridges. Geologists were always a bit wary of this sort of bridge building, but biologists felt it necessary in order to account for numerous species of plants and animals that occurred on both sides of the Atlantic. Today, most of these parallels can be accounted for in other ways.

Most geologists now lean toward the theory of continental drift, to explain the placement of the land masses of the earth. This theory holds that all the earth's land was once clumped into one or two great supercontinents. These split up and moved slowly into the places they now occupy. Continental drift is not a new theory; it was first proposed by the German meteorologist Alfred Wegener in 1912. But it did not gain favor at the time. It was not enough simply to say that the continents moved; there had to be some reasonable proposal concerning the forces which moved them, and in 1912 there was none available.

Then in the late 1950s oceanographers discovered that the Atlantic and Pacific oceans are split by great subterranean ridges; indeed, the entire world seems to be rent by a network of such ridges. These ridges are cracks which reach deep beneath the crust of the earth to the mantle, where the pressure is so great that the rock is hot enough to be in a molten or plastic state. This is the part of the earth from which the lava of volcanoes erupts. A certain amount of this hot interior material is constantly welling up from the ridges, and it creates the pressure which pushes the great blocks of the continental land masses apart. The ridges themselves are thought to be the meeting place of upward-moving currents within the plastic mantle. One facet of the theory is that there has never been a significant difference in the amount of continental land.

The continental drift theory as presented here is vastly simplified and far from proved. The only thing we can be absolutely certain of is that the ridges do exist. But as far as Atlantis is concerned, the discoveries of the last twenty years make it less likely than ever that there was an unknown continent in the middle of the Atlantic Ocean.

We have to face the more than real possibility that Plato simply made up the whole Atlantis story and that the centuries-long search for the lost continent has been a complete waste of time. After all, Plato had constructed other imaginary places to illustrate his philosophical points. No one has ever thought it necessary to find the location of Plato's famous cave, which he used to illustrate many of his ideas about the nature of the universe.

But there remains a third possibility. The basis for Plato's Atlantis story may lie in some real, though relatively minor catastrophe, which the philosopher expanded into the story of the sinking of a continent.

Numerous disasters have been proposed to account for Atlantis. Poet and classical scholar Robert Graves traces at least part of the story to the sinking of the small island of

Pharos in the mouth of the Nile River. L. Sprague de Camp, compiler of one of the few truly scientific works on Atlantis, *Lost Continents*, believes that Tartessos, "the Biblical Tarshish, Jonah's destination," was the inspiration for the story. Tartessos was a flourishing city-state in southwestern Spain. Somewhere around 500 B.C. Tartessos simply drops out of history. No one knows what happened to it, and very few relics from it have ever been located. The Carthaginians told wondrous tales about it, and perhaps they destroyed it because it was a commercial rival.

Says de Camp, "Tartessos, like Atlantis, lay in the far west beyond the Pillars; it was enormously rich, especially in minerals, and had wide commercial contacts with the Mediterranean; it was associated with shoals; behind it lay a great plain bordered by mountains; and it mysteriously disappeared. While the Tartessians are not known to have performed a bull-ceremony, the region was and still is a cattle country. No one knows what fate befell Tartessos, but its ruins are today sunk deep in the mud, for it once stood at the mouth of a river that has long since silted up."

For centuries Atlantis has been almost the sole province of crankish scholarship. But in 1967 a group of perfectly respectable scientists seriously announced that they had found Atlantis. It was not a sunken continent in the Atlantic. What they had found was evidence that a great natural catastrophe may have destroyed a civilization that could be related to Atlantis.

Somewhere about 1400 B.C. the volcanic island of Santorini in the Aegean Sea blew apart with unprecedented fury. Ash from the explosion has been detected over an 80,000-square-mile area.

Only the barest outline of the effects of this ancient explosion have been reconstructed, but a good deal can be learned by comparing the explosion of Santorini with the explosion of the East Indian volcanic island of Krakatoa in 1883. The 1460-foot volcano of Krakatoa exploded with such force that rocks were thrown fifty miles, and so much dust was shot into the atmosphere that sunsets around the world were unusually red for a full year. The spent volcano collapsed in upon itself, generating tidal waves that destroyed hundreds of villages and drowned some 36,000 people. Four hundred and eighty miles away from Krakatoa, houses shook from the noise, and two thousand miles away it could still be heard. The explosion of Santorini must have been considerably worse.

That there had been a cataclysmic explosion of Santorini at some point was well known. The volcanic ash makes an excellent quality of waterproof cement and has been mined for that puropse for over a hundred years. A lot of it was used in building the Suez Canal. But the date of the explosion could not be fixed until 1956 when Professor Angelos Galanopoulos, of the Athens Seismological Institute, made an astonishing discovery on the island of Thera, one of the bits of the Santorini crater that had not sunk after the explosion. At the bottom of a mine shaft he found the ruins of a stone house, and from wood and bone in the house he was able to date its destruction to the fifteenth century B.C. The house lay under one hundred feet of volcanic ash. Krakatoa, in contrast, deposited only about one foot of ash.

The date was a surprise, and it made the explosion of Santorini an historical and archaeological, as well as a geological, problem. Santorini is quite close to Greece and even closer to the island of Crete. About 1400 B.C. Crete was the home of the Minoans, one of the most brilliant and enigmatic civilizations of the ancient world.

The Greeks had legends about Crete and its powerful ruler King Minos, but no one in modern times believed the legends until 1900, when Sir Arthur Evans began digging up palaces and temples on Crete. These proved that Crete had possessed a very ancient and very advanced civilization. The Minoans, as the people of ancient Crete are called, must have ruled the Aegean while the Greeks were still barbarians.

But Minoan civilization vanished abruptly and mysteriously, and Crete was overrun by Greek-speaking people from the mainland, whom we call Mycenaeans. The Mycenaeans were the people Homer wrote about, a hardy, vigorous bronze age warrior society.

In the *Iliad* and the *Odyssey*, Crete is described as just another Greek city state. But other legends of Minos tell of a time when fleets from the island ruled the Aegean and were able to extract tribute even from Athens. Those same legends hint at the great antiquity of the people of Crete. Zeus, king of the gods, was reputed to have been born there, and later he carried the nymph Europa to the island. Europa, of course, gave Europe its name, and since Evans' discoveries, the island of Crete, home of Europa and Zeus, is also considered to be home of the earliest all truly European civilizations.

In the 1960s Professor Galanopoulos and a number of his Greek and American colleagues began investigating the explosion of Santorini more thoroughly. In 1967 they announced their most spectacular discovery: the ruins of a virtually intact Minoan city had been located under the centuries-old ash of Thera. Archaeologists have calculated that the city covered about half a square mile. It was made up mostly of humble dwellings, closely spaced two- and three-story structures, although one luxurious abode, perhaps the villa of a nobleman, has also been located. The total population of the town may have been as high as thirty thousand. Some investigators believe that there may be other towns buried under the volcanic debris.

The discovery on Thera is sure to rank as one of the greatest ever made anywhere, because the buried town itself is so well preserved.

Unlike the destruction by volcano of the Roman cities of Pompeii and Herculaneum which was sudden, the scientific estimate is that there was plenty of warning for the people who lived on Santorini. The build-up of ash is so deep that there must have been initial minor explosions, and pumice and ash may have belched forth for as long as fifty years before the final overwhelming catastrophe.

At Pompeii you can find evidence of the speed of the disaster. Men and women were caught in the rain of hot ashes, and as the ash solidified, it formed a cast of the bodies, preserving their final death agony. No such grisly souvenirs occur on Thera. Apparently the people of the doomed island heeded the warning and fled. So far only two human skeletons have been found, although the remains of animals are numerous. No gold or other precious objects have turned up either. The refugees took their valuable with them.

But what they left behind is in a magnificent state of preservation. In the limited amount of digging that has gone on so far, painted frescoes have been found, and archaeologists look forward to finding a wealth of paintings.

Volcanic ash filled the buildings and acted as excelsior in a packing crate, preventing them from crumbling in the earth shocks that followed the explosion. Even huge pottery jars for the storage of oil and wine were dug unbroken from the ash.

Under other circumstances they would have been smashed to fragments.

Santorini was overwhelmed, and part of it sank during a catastrophe of unprecedented magnitude. Professor Galanopoulos and his colleagues believe that this was the event which inspired Plato's Atlantis. The descriptions of the sacred precincts of Atlantis, with its hot springs and circular canals, "fits perfectly the features, shape and size of the island of Santorini," says Galanopoulos. "Traces of the canals and harbors are discernible even now on the floor of the caldera, or undersea crater."

The Atlantis legend Galanopoulos believes refers to more than the destruction of Santorini; it must allude to the fall of Minoan civilization, which in the view of the Greek scientist was the direct result of the Santorini explosion.

The tidal waves and shock waves generated by the principal explosion must have had a profound effect on nearby Crete. If Krakatoa is any guide, the Santorini explosion created havoc in Greece, Egypt, Palestine and all the other lands around the Aegean-Mediterranean area. Most of the damage was temporary, but the explosion probably finished the Minoans. Carried by prevailing southeasterly winds, the volcanic fallout from Santorini was blown to Crete, where it filled the fertile valleys and literally smothered Minoan agriculture. The once mighty Minoan fleets had undoubtedly been smashed to matchwood by the tidal waves. A battered and exhausted Minoan race was wide open for the invasion of the Mycenaeans, who had suffered relatively little as a result of the explosion.

The Greeks of the time, so this theory runs, were a barbaric people, unlikely to retain a clear record of even so frightful a catastrophe. The Egyptians would probably have a clearer recollection. The Minoan empire was well known to the Egyptians. This makes the incident of Solon getting the Atlantis tale from an Egyptian priest sound more sensible. Surviving Egyptian records don't contain any clear references to the explosion, but Galanopoulous believes that the Biblical descriptions of the events surrounding the Exodus of the children of Israel from Egypt may in a fanciful way tell of the chain of events which were set off by the explosion of Santorini. The darkness, the noise, the winds, the wave that drowned Pharaoh and his army, all may have come from the volcanic cataclysm taking place 450 miles away from the delta of the Nile. But the problem of Exodus can be and has been debated endlessly. Let's stick with Atlantis; it presents enough problems.

The main objection to the Galanopoulos theory is that the Minoan civilization was too small, too new, and too close to Greece to square away with Plato's Atlantis. The Greek seismologist has a ready answer. Solon, or at least some Greek along the line, misread the Egyptian symbol for 100 as 1000 and every number in the Atlantis story became multiplied tenfold. Knock all the figures down to a tenth their size and you have the sinking of Atlantis taking place nine hundred years before Solon—in the fifteenth century B.C. The size would be on the order of 80,000 square miles, an acceptable estimate of the lands under Minoan domination. And Galanopoulos notes triumphantly the Strait of Gibralter is not the only Pillars of Hercules; there are two promontories on the coast of Greece facing Crete that also carry that name.

Do you want more parallels between the Minoans and the Atlanteans? They abound. Atlantis and Athens were rivals;

the legend of the hero Theseus indicates that Crete and Athens were great rivals. The Atlanteans were great seafarers; so were the Minoans. Plato specifically mentions the bull as an object of worship; Theseus had to destroy the Minotaur, a monster, half bull, half man, and excavations on Crete have turned up a large number of bull symbols. The Athenians alone stood against the Atlanteans; Theseus was a prince of Athens, and the only one with the courage to challenge Minos. He also overcame Minos, which may be a mythological rendition of the real invasion of Crete by mainland Greeks.

At least one historian has said, "It seems that the riddle of Atlantis has finally been solved."

It would be satisfying to wrap up all the puzzles about Atlantis and for that matter about the Minoans and attribute them to the explosion of Santorini, but it would also be premature. For this explanation to be acceptable, we have to assume that Minoan civilization was abruptly cut off 1400 B.C. The date is possible but by no means firm. A recent reexamination of Arthur Evans' original notes of his excavations on Crete has led at least one prominent scholar to say that the Minoans were invaded from the Greek mainland and fell in 1200 B.C. Evans believed that some sort of catastrophe (he favored an earthquake) triggered the end of the kingdom of Minos; others are not so sure. It may have been the invasion, an internal revolution, or just old age. Many see in the Minoan remains evidence of a beautiful and cultivated people, but others see in the elaborate luxury an overcultivated decadent civilization ready to collapse.

Too much speculation at this point is foolish and unnecessary. Excavations at Thera and Crete will undoubtedly throw new light on the mysteries of the Minoans.

Even if the Minoan excavations do turn up more evidence

to support the already impressive case that the sinking of Atlantis was inspired by the Santorini explosion and the fall of Crete, it will not end the search for Atlantis—the other Atlantis, which will rise again.

TWO

LEMURIA

The Atlantis of the Pacific

The legend of Lemuria got its start in the human longing for symmetry. The Greeks knew the world was round, and they were familiar with one quarter of the globe, a quarter extraordinarily well filled with land. It was natural to assume that the other three quarters had equal amounts of land.

The voyages of Columbus and the other great seafarers of the fifteenth and sixteenth centuries punctured the old ideas about the shape and size of the earth, but still people could never quite get over the idea that the earth should be more symmetrical—at least there should be as much land below the equator as there is above. Nature is not bound by such conventions and has been very sloppy and unsymmetrical in the placement of land. The combined continents of Asia and Europe are entirely in the Northern Hemisphere. North America is larger in land area than South America. Moreover, neither South America nor Africa lie entirely south of the equator. The Southern Hemisphere has only the small continents of Australia and Antarctica, and a number of tiny islands.

Before this was known, however, when Europeans first began to penetrate the waters of the South Pacific, they expected to find a large continent there, somewhere beyond the west coast of South America. Mapmakers often put in an ill-defined land mass, which they labeled *Terra Australis Incognita*, or "the great unknown southern continent."

In 1576 Juan Fernandez returned to South America after a sojourn in the South Pacific with the report that he had discovered a large well-watered continent, inhabited by prosperous, well-dressed white men. Fernandez may have sighted Easter Island, but the rest of the story is sheer imagination.

The Portuguese must have spotted Australia often during their voyages to the Malay Archipelago in the sixteenth century—indeed it is hard to see how they could have missed it—but there is no record of such sightings. The first to land on the island continent were the Dutch in the early part of the seventeenth century. They called it New Holland.

Two hundred years later the South Pacific had been criss-crossed so many times without finding the great unknown southern continent that even the die-hards had to admit it wasn't there. The great navigator Captain James Cook claimed the little continent, which he called Australia, for the British. It was a great disappointment. Hot, dry, without gold, without cities of civilized white men and with natives so poor they were hardly worth robbing, it was deemed a place fit only for convicts and other outcasts.

But a concept that was once accepted as enthusiastically as that of a southern continent never dies entirely. Over the centuries the great unknown southern continent has bobbed up again, and again, under a variety of names, for a variety of reasons. Of course, it was no longer an existing continent but one that had somehow or other been "lost," a sort of Atlantis of the Pacific.

Oddly, the most familiar name for this lost Pacific continent, Lemuria, was a by-product of the controversy which greeted the publication of Charles Darwin's *The Origin of Species*. Darwin's opponents, who held that all species had been specially created and were eternally unchanged, had a simple way of explaining how similar creatures got to widely scattered parts of the earth: "God put them there." Evolutionists had a more difficult task. If similar species had evolved in one place from a common ancestor, then they must have had some physical means of crossing vast areas of ocean. Particularly vexing was the problem of the lemur, a small primitive form of primate, found in abundance on the island of Madagascar but also found throughout Africa, India and the Malay Archipelago. Some zoologists suggested that all these areas were once connected in one vast continent, which existed well into the time when mammals were evolving. An English zoologist, Philip L. Schlater, proposed the name "Lemuria" for this continent.

It was a German naturalist, Ernst Heinrich Haeckel, who gave Lemuria its real push into fame as a lost continent. Darwin himself was a cautious retiring man, who shunned controversy and elaborate speculation. Many of his followers were of a very different character. Reckless, belligerent, often unfair and wildly wrong in their enthusiasm, they did perform the great service of literally forcing the theory of evolution upon the world. Every country had its advocate of Darwin. In England it was Thomas Henry Huxley, "Darwin's bulldog," in America it was Othniel Charles Marsh, and in Germany, Ernst Heinrich Haeckel.

Haeckel used Lemuria not only to explain the ubiquity of lemurs, but also to solve an even more troublesome problem for the evolutionists. Although the fossil remains of many creatures had been found, no fossil remains of man had been found when the great controversy over evolution was at its height. (Actually, a portion of the skull of a Neanderthal man had been discovered, but it was sitting, unidentified, in a museum in Germany. Other unidentified Neanderthal fragments turned up later in other collections.)

Haeckel wrote: "Of the five now existing continents, neither Australia nor America nor Europe can have been this primeval home (of man), or the so-called 'Paradise' the 'cradle of the human race.' Besides Southern Asia, the only other of the now existing continents which might be viewed in this light is Africa. But there are a number of circumstances (especially chronological facts), which suggest that the primeval home of man was a continent now sunk below the surface of the Indian Ocean, which extended along the south of Asia, as it is at present (and probably in direct connection with it), towards the east, as far as Further India and the Sunda Islands; towards the west, as far as Madagascar and the south-eastern shores of Africa. We have already mentioned that many facts in animal and vegetable geography render the former existence of such a South Indian continent very probable. Schlater has given this continent the name of Lemuria, from the semi-apes which were characteristic of it. By assuming this Lemuria to have been man's primeval home, we greatly facilitate the explanation of the geographical distribution of the human species by migration."

No less a figure than Alfred Russel Wallace, the man who had independently developed the theory of evolution at the same time as Darwin, considered Lemuria "a legitimate and highly probable suggestion." He later retreated from this position.

Thomas Henry Huxley, as skeptical a man as ever lived, wrote in 1880, "There is nothing, so far as I am aware, in the biological evidence at present accessible, to render untenable the hypothesis that an area of the mid-Atlantic or Pacific sea bed as big as Europe should have been uplifted as high as Mont Blanc, and have subsided again any time since the Palaeozoic epoch, if there were any grounds for entertaining it." An uncharacteristically cautious statement from a man who had a habit of smashing any ideas he deemed foolish. Lemuria, and Atlantis, for that matter, were not considered at all foolish in 1880.

It is notable, though, that the most enthusiastic support for Lemuria and other sunken continents came from biologists, who were looking for a convenient bridge by which animals could wander from place to place. Geologists were more reticent, for they could not easily conceive of the forces which could raise and lower enormous land masses in such a relatively short time. Some geologists, however, pointed out the resemblance between rock and fossil formations in a part of India called Gondwana, and a deposit from the same period in southern Africa. The name Gondwana means "Land of the Gonds," a tribe that inhabited the area. Gondwanaland was the name applied to a theoretical gigantic supercontinent that either stretched three quarters of the way around the Southern Hemisphere, or represented a clumping together of most of the present continents. The number depends upon which authority is doing the theorizing. Since it was proposed back in the middle of the nineteenth century, the concept of Gondwanaland had only marginal support among geologists until recent years. Dramatic discoveries in the last few years, however, have strongly indicated that all the southern continents probably were once connected, and broke apart and drifted away from one another. But if this happened, it happened long before man appeared on the face of the earth and thus has nothing to do with the popular search for the lost continent of Lemuria.

In the years that followed the origination of the concept of Lemuria, the lost continent moved up in time. Supporters placed Lemuria's submergence anywhere from the late stone age to the middle of the seventeenth century. They moved the geographical position of Lemuria too. Whereas it once connected Africa and Asia, so the lemurs could walk comfortably from one to the other, later supporters of the continent put it out in the middle of the South Pacific, the area where the waves are now broken only by a scattering of small islands. Some saw these islands as the tops of the mountains of the drowned continent. Even when these theories about the Pacific Lemuria were first proposed, they were geologically untenable, and in light of our vastly increased knowledge about the structure of the oceans and continents today, they are even more so.

This, however, had not the slightest effect on the army of speculators who have propounded elaborate theories on the structure of Lemuria, the culture of its inhabitants, and the reasons for its demise.

In his *Riddle of the Pacific*, published early in this century, Professor J. Macmillan Brown of Christchurch, New Zealand, brought together a smattering of geology, archaeology and anthropology to prove the former existence of a great continent in the Pacific. If it was not a single continent, then it was at least a densely populated archipelago, ruled by an industrious race of white men. Easter Island served as the collective burial place for the people of the neighboring islands. Professor Brown places the final disappearance of his archipelago between 1687 and 1722. He has been described by one critic as "a man with a mind both simple and excessively imaginative."

Yet, Professor Brown anticipated many of the theories of Thor Heyerdahl of Kon Tiki fame. Like Heyerdahl, Professor Brown saw many significant similarities between the monuments and customs of the people of Polynesia and those of South America, particularly the civilizations of Peru. But while Heyerdahl saw the people of South America bringing their culture to the islands of Polynesia, Professor Brown saw the movement going the other direction from Polynesia, or rather Lemuria, to South America.

One of the most careful, moderate and scholarly of the authentic Lemuria enthusiasts was Lewis Spence, the Scottish mythologist. Spence's attitude toward Lemuria was much the same as his attitude toward Atlantis; he rejected the wilder claims of the occultists, who were able to reconstruct the entire history of the continent by a variety of meditations, yet he could not rid himself of the idea that a great continent had sunk, bringing disaster and dispersal to a great race. Nor could he ever overcome the desire to shake off the chains of fact and soar freely in the realm of pure imagination.

In his book *The Problem of Lemuria* Spence sums up his feelings thus:

"The question as to whether Lemuria disappeared wholly or partially is almost unnecessary to pose when so many insular evidences of its former existence remain. Indeed, I have some difficulty in comprehending the kind of mentality which can view a map of Oceania (Australia and the islands of the South Pacific)—filled as it is with insular groups—without almost at once agreeing with the hypothesis of the former existence of great land masses in an area so vast. Seriously are we to suppose that of all the earth's regions this alone, with the exception of the Atlantic, was destitute of continental land, especially when we behold the evidence of the mountain peaks of that land still littering a space occupying so many thousands of miles?"

Spence continues: "The day is passing when mere weight of evidence alone, unsupported by considerations which result from inspiration and insight, can be accepted of the world, which indeed is weary of the blundering processes of that species of thought which refuses to avail itself of those intuitional gifts without which real knowledge and progress can never be accomplished."

Earnest, rather admirable, dogmatic, and more than a little foolish, Spence's credo could be used by all the romantic seekers after lost lands.

Spence believed the evidence for Lemuria was much stronger than that for the more famous Atlantis. Spence believed Lemuria did not collapse and sink in a single terrifying catastrophe, a favorite theme among lost-land lovers. Rather, it crumbled slowly over a period of many years. What of the people? "It must also be clear," Spence writes, "that any wild theories regarding its occupation by a race with superhuman attributes cannot be entertained." Spence's Lemuria was a land of many races, but naturally the white race was the Lemurian aristocracy and "the conservators of all hidden knowledge and magic."

Spence believed that white refugees from Lemuria brought civilization to the Indians of South America. He supported this belief by relating the many tales of white gods who brought civilization to the Mayas, Aztecs and Incas. "The legends relating to a fair civilizing race cannot but apply to a white Lemurian aristocracy." Europeans, of course, were the truest descendants of the Lemurian aristocracy.

The most persistent and interesting of the legends of a white civilizer among the Indians are those which relate to the Central American god Quetzalcoatl. Yet, in another part to *The Problem of Lemuria* Spence describes Quetzalcoatl as "decidedly Buddhistic in his aspect and insignia, as well as in the traditions which relate to him." Quetzalcoatl, he believed, was a Buddhist missionary come to civilize the heathens. Presumably the missionary's trip across the Pacific was made much easier because he could traverse a good part of the distance on land, the now sunken Lemuria.

Spence cites legends which have Quetzalcoatl appearing from the East. But interpreters, eager to prove that the inspiration for Central and South American civilizations came from Europe, find equally good evidence in the same set of legends that he came from the West. Those elements that Spence finds "decidedly Buddhistic," others have found decidedly western, even Christian. Using this sort of evidence, a diligent Chinese scholar could build an impressive case for his homeland being the cradle of American pre-Columbian civilization in just the same way as many diligent persons of European descent have built a similar case for their homeland.

Actually, in the early days of the rediscovery of the Indian civilizations of Central and South America, and for that matter even in the early speculations concerning the great mounds built by the Indians of North America, the idea that they had somehow drawn direct inspiration from Asia was very much in vogue. Explorers found pictures of "undoubted elephants" on the walls of Maya temples, and discovered "Chinese sculpture" scattered throughout Central America.

Lemuria figured heavily in all this speculation for its existence made an otherwise arduous sea trip from Asia much more feasible.

Unsupportable as some of these speculations may sound today, they represent a serious, if misguided, attempt to deal with Lemuria in terms of observable facts. But within two decades after the concept of Lemuria was evolved by the biologists, it was enthusiastically adopted by the occultists. They peopled the land of the lemurs with exotic beings and made it the home of all manner of mysterious wisdom, to which they and they alone held the key.

Spence is scornful of most of the occult theorists, but he is clearly awed by the greatest of them all, Madame Helena Petrovna Blavatsky, the founder of Theosophy. He writes of her, "It would be merely foolish to deny (that she) was a most distinguished student of the arcane, and everything she wrote was characterized, as a general rule, by logic and temperate statement. So much one is bound to admit in homage to a great mind."

In reality H.P.B., as she was known to her friends, was a fantastic charlatan, in the grand tradition of St. Germain and Cagliostro. To call her anything else would be insulting, and would doubtless have earned you a great horselaugh from the madame herself. She never made any big secret of the amount of nonsense she had managed to put over on the world.

H.P.B. elaborated her Lemurian ideas in *The Secret Doctrine*, a book of impressive length and unbelievable obscurity. She claimed to have learned of Lemuria in *The Book of Dzyan*, which was composed in Atlantis and shown to her by the mysterious Mahatmas. *The Book of Dzyan*, it seems, was entirely a product of the madame's active imagination. The real sources for *The Secret Doctrine* were the scientific and pseudoscientific writings of the day mixed in with occult meanderings and translations of Oriental religious works. She cribbed freely, inaccurately and without credit, although she gave Philip Schlater the dubious honor of being the man who invented the name Lemuria.

According to H.P.B., Lemuria, at one time or another, covered virtually every part of the globe; it all depends on which page of *The Secret Doctrine* you happen to be reading. "It is a little baffling to read that Scandinavia formed part of Lemuria and also of Atlantis 'on the European side,'" says the genuinely puzzled Spence.

It is useless, and probably impossible, to attempt a point by point refutation of the Lemurian speculations of *The Secret Doctrine*. The book is a mishmash, set down in extreme haste, by a cynically clever woman who knew full well that most of those who bought the book would not attempt to criticize it, understand it, or even read it, but would be satisfyingly impressed by its length and by the number of strange words it contained.

Madame Blatvatsky's Lemurians were the third root race to inhabit the earth. The first lived on an Imperishable Sacred Land, the second in the Arctic continent of Hyperborea. The fourth root race were the Atlanteans. We are the fifth. The Lemurians had a "third eye" which gave them psychic vision. They seemed to need no brain or "any physical vehicle to attain connection with the spirit." Despite this apparently insubstantial form they were described as gigantic, apelike, egg-laying bisexuals, and their downfall seems somehow to be connected with their discovery of sex. One unkind but accurate critic has noted "H.P.B. took a dim view of sex after she reached the age when she herself was no longer interested in it."

After the world-wide catastrophe, the Lemurians "gravitated to the North Pole" or the Hyperborean continent, and the Atlanteans to the South Pole. There they mated with "animals," possibly producing the forerunners of man. With H.P.B. it is hard to be sure exactly what she meant, or if she meant anything at all.

At a later date in her monthly publication, *The Theosophist*, she wrote more clearly: "There are or were, descendants of these half-animal tribes or races of remote Lemurian origin, Tasmanians, Australians, Andaman Islanders, etc. The Lemurians, in some cases, were gigantic and bestial and begat a species which later developed into 'mammalian apes.'"

Madame Blavatsky's most illustrious successor, Annie Besant, provided more details on the appearance of the typical Lemurian. He was between twelve and fifteen feet tall, with long arms which could not be completely straightened. He could walk equally well backward or forward, owning to heels which stuck out as far to the rear of his foot as his toes did in the front. He was brown-skinned, flat-faced but possessed a definite muzzle, and lacked a forehead. His two usual eyes were set so wide apart that he could see equally well ahead or to the side. His third eye can still be found in vestigial form among humans in the pineal gland in the brain. His clothes were made of reptile skin, and he made pets of dinosaurs.

The last of the great occult speculators on the lost Pacific continent was James Churchward, who rose to popularity in America in the 1920s and 1930s. Churchward had another name for his Pacific continent; he called it Mu.

Churchward did not invent the name. He got it from two

eccentric French scholars, Abbé Charles-Étienne Brasseur de Bourbourg and Augustus Le Plongeon. Both men believed the Indian civilizations of Central America came from a land called Mu, which they identified with Atlantis.

On the basis of some "Naacal Tablets" which he claimed to have discovered in a monastery in India, Churchward came to a somewhat different conclusion about Mu:

"The Garden of Eden was not in Asia but on a now sunken continent in the Pacific Ocean. The Biblical story of creation— the epic of the seven days and the seven nights—came first not from the peoples of the Nile or the Euphrates Valley but from this now submerged continent—the Motherland of Man."

Churchward basically professed a sort of eccentric religious fundamentalism. (He stood foursquare against "monkey evolution.") But he attempted to give his series of books about "the Motherland of Man" the look of works of genuine archaeological research. However, he quoted with equal vigor from archaeologists, occultists, frauds and even writers of imaginative fiction like H. Rider Haggard. Churchward's books were handsomely produced and filled with drawings, diagrams and footnotes. Unfortunately the drawings and diagrams are often inaccurate or meaningless, and the footnotes like "Lhasa records and others" and "Maya and others" are no help at all to the scholar trying to track down the sources of Churchward's remarkable information. Other footnotes like "Troanto Manuscript" and "Easter Island Tablet" refer to documents that have never been translated except, presumably, by Churchward himself, which means that you simply have to take his word for it.

Churchward not only disbelieved in biological evolution, he also disbelieved in cultural evolution. "At this time the people of Mu were highly civilized and enlightened. There was no savagery on the face of the earth nor had there ever been, since all the peoples of the earth were children of Mu and under the suzerainty of the motherland."

As was common in his day (and all too common in our own), Churchward was eager to pick up the white man's burden. "The dominant race in the land of Mu was a white race, exceedingly handsome people, with clear white or olive skins, large, soft, dark eyes and straight black hair. Besides this white race there were other races, people with yellow, brown and black skins. They, however, did not dominate."

He collects all the old tales of white Indians, white Asians, white Africans, and white ruling races from every part of the globe to build his case. He even adds a few "traditions" which originated in his own head. "The Chinese civilization is referred to and looked upon as one of the very old ones. As a Chinese civilization it dates back only about 5000 years. It is popularly believed that the Chinese themselves developed their civilization. They did not. The Chinese civilization was inherited from their father's side. Again, the Chinaman is looked upon as a Mongol; he is only half Mongol, his forefathers were white Aryans."

Churchward says the earth was once honeycombed with vast subterranean chambers filled with volcanic gas. "These gas chambers were the final assassins of Mu," he wrote. The gas escaped through volcanic action, the chambers collapsed, and Mu sank, scattering her children throughout the rest of the earth to form all the civilizations we know today.

Yet another name for the lost Pacific continent was Pan. This was the creation of John Ballou, a Newburgh, New York, dentist and spiritualist. Ballou said that he had been angelically inspired to write a new bible he called *Oahspe*. Like all books produced by automatic writing, *Oahspe* is very long and virtually unreadable. But through the murky language one can discern the usual theme of the supremacy of the white race. Along with a map of Pan, which is shown as a triangular continent in the northern Pacific, Ballou presents his history of the races of mankind. The angels appeared on earth and mated with a strange seal-like animal, the A'su, to produce the I'hins. The I'hins and the A'su recrossed to beget the Druk. Africans and Asians are the remnants of the Druks, but the white race was produced by another mating between the Druk and the I'hins, making them one step closer to the angels than the colored races.

Lemuria surfaced once again in the mid-1940s. It was a boom time for pulp science fiction magazines and the gaudiest of the remarkable collection of magazines published then were *Amazing Stories* and *Fantastic Adventures*, edited by Raymond A. Palmer. Starting in March 1945 and continuing for three years, Palmer published a series of stories by Richard S. Shaver, a Pennsylvania welder. The first of the stories, "I Remember Lemuria," told of the previous condition of the earth when Atlantis and Lemuria still towered above the waves. In many respects the Shaver stories were pretty standard stuff for science fiction magazines. The difference was that both Shaver and Palmer claimed they were truth not fiction. Shaver wrote that in the good old days earth was inhabited by the great races of the Titans and Atlans, but they were forced to flee the planet, leaving behind the human race and the deros. The deros were evil creatures who crept about subterranean caverns messing up the human race by telepathically implanting bad thoughts in our heads.

Shaver claimed that he got his information for these stories through "racial memory." Admirers called the stories "The Great Shaver Mystery." Detractors, and there were plenty among science fiction fans and writers who like to draw a clear line between fiction and fact, called them "The Great Shaver Hoax." Now, more than twenty years after the series began, both Shaver and Palmer still claim they were true stories, although a certain coolness seems to have grown up between them. In 1967 Shaver wrote, "He [Palmer] changed my 'Warning to Future Man' into an occult slant giving it the title 'I Remember Lemuria' (Palmer has always had this occult bug on everything). And from there on I fought against this misinterpretation of my work from the practical research into the remnants of the past, that it was, from Palmer's picture of my work as 'occult' insight into the past."

Palmer still often speaks of the evil influence the deros are having on him and cancels engagements at the last minute because of some interference of the deros. One gets the really uncomfortable feeling that these tales of Lemuria were not the result of a conscious hoax, or if they were, the chief victims have been the men who concocted it.

So there is the curious history of Lemuria or the great unknown southern continent. Since it had so little grounding in fact, or even in genuine ancient tradition, it slipped most easily from the realm of reasonable speculation into murky occultism. But there it lives, and prospers after a fashion. You can buy paperback editions of Churchward's books at many bookstores. Theosophy is not what it once was but it is still very much around. There are even little groups that meet to discuss "The Great Shaver Mystery."

THREE

EASTER ISLAND

Puzzle of the Pacific

In 1687 the English privateer Edward Davis was sailing along the west coast of South America when his ship was caught in high winds and blown several hundred miles out to sea. Far out in the Pacific he sighted land where no land had ever been reported before. He saw a sandy beach, and in the background were the silhouettes of high mountains. Davis did not bother to see how large an area of land he had sighted, he swung his ship eastward and headed for Peru.

Davis probably sighted Easter Island and could well have been the first European ever to do so. When an account of Davis' sighting was published, many believed he had sighted the edge of "the great unknown southern continent."

When Ferdinand Magellan sailed around South America he believed he had caught sight of part of the continent. He named it Tierra del Fuego, "Land of Fire," a name inspired by his glimpsing the campfires of the natives. Tierra del Fuego turned out to be an island. Indeed, the area of the unknown continent turned out to be dotted with innumerable islands, and one genuine continent, Australia. After Captain James Cook landed in Australia, the belief that a much larger continent had been overlooked persisted. Cook sailed back and forth over the unfriendly seas that were supposed to contain this continent, without ever finding it.

If the continent could not be found, some reasoned, it was because it had disappeared. No lost land ever becomes popular without stories of the supercivilization that existed upon it. So the idea of wonders to be found in the South Pacific lasted into the eighteenth century. They needed only a spot to which to attach themselves. This spot turned out to be the misty "Davis Land" or, as it is known today, Easter Island.

Unfortunately for the romantics, geology gives not the slightest support to the idea that Easter Island ever was part of a sunken continent. Quite the contrary, soundings indicate that the water for a ten-mile radius around the isolated island is extremely deep, averaging 1,145 fathoms.

Easter Island, like Tahiti, the Hawaiian Islands, and others of the South Pacific, is the result of fairly recent volcanic eruptions. Continental land masses are made up of a particular type of rock, but extensive analysis of the rocks of Easter Island have not turned up any continental formations. All the material is derived from the eruptions of now extinct volcanoes.

Therefore, geologically speaking, Easter Island is young, built up from eruptions just a few millennia ago, but this was long before man ever set foot on the island. Could volcanic activity in recent times have destroyed the larger part of the island and disrupted a flourishing civilization? Geologists say no recent cataclysm has struck Easter Island. But that it is being destroyed no one can deny. The action of weather and waves upon the soft volcanic material is wearing away the land.

One day Easter Island will indeed disappear beneath the waves. The disintegration is measurable along the shore line. A few thousand years from now the only reminder of the island will be the skeletons of corals that have built a reef on the submerged volcanic crater. The island's nearest neighbor, Sala y Gómez, 210 miles away, has been reduced to such a reef, a fit home only for the far-ranging sea birds.

The nearest inhabited island is Pitcairn, 1200 miles to the east. This is the island upon which the mutineers of the *Bounty* chose to hide themselves. To the west, 2000 miles of open ocean separates Easter Island from the coast of Chile.

By no stretch of the imagination can Easter Island be described as a tropical paradise. It is only fifty square miles, much of it boulder-covered fields which make walking difficult. From the sea the cones of Rano Raraku, Rano Kao and Rano Aroi, three extinct volcanoes, are the most obvious features.

The climate is mild, but colder than a tropical paradise should be. Winds are strong and constant. Before the coming of man there were no mammals on the island, but the winds had blown insects from distant shores, and they have prospered to the point where they are a considerable nuisance today. The ever-present salty winds and the thin soil make it impossible for any tall plants, including trees, to grow there. Easter Island has no fresh-water rivers or streams. There are lakes in the craters of the extinct volcanoes, but these are difficult to reach. Rain falls often enough, but it quickly sinks through the porous soil, so that obtaining an adequate supply of fresh water is a constant problem.

Life on the island is hard, but possible. Today the island supports a population of about one thousand but at one time the population may have been six times as large.

The reason this unattractive bit of real estate has become the object of fascination for the entire world is because at one time the people of Easter Island indulged, with great vigor, in building colossal monuments—the famous Easter Island "heads." "These so-called statues," says Alfred Metraux, member of a 1934 French Expedition to the Island, "are, in fact, enormous busts, monstrous legless cripples with heads too long for their massive trunks."

Originally there were hundreds of them. The most finished were placed in sacred enclosures along the coast. Another 250 to 300 were set up on the slopes of Rano Raraku. Others scattered about seem to have once marked roads. Nearly two hundred unfinished statues are still in the quarry.

The largest of the finished statues is thirty-three feet high and twenty-five feet eight inches around its widest place. It was once surmounted by a cylindrical "hat" six feet high and eight feet across. Even larger colossi, including one sixty-six feet long, remain in the quarry.

Though badly battered, the statues are impressive. Writes Metraux: "During the three weeks we lived among the statues we saw them in sunshine, by moonlight, and on stormy nights. Each time we felt the same shock, the same uneasiness, as on the first day. This sense of oppression is due less to their dimensions than to their confused distribution. If they were arranged in some apparent order one could catch a glimpse of the purpose and plan of the dead; but the almost human casualness and turbulence with which this assembly of giants with huge noses and flat necks is scattered about is somehow disturbing."

Metraux speaks of "the plan of the dead" although the direct descendants of the statue builders still inhabit Easter Island. But the culture which produced the statues is as dead as if the island had sunk and the inhabitants drowned to a man. The impact of European explorers, slavers and missionaries was more profound, and destructive to the peoples of the South Sea Islands, than anywhere on earth. Island life was tenuous at best. The island populations were small and life was primitive. The people could not fight, could not hide from and could not endure what Alan Moorehead has called "the fatal impact" of the coming of the white man.

Of all the peoples of Oceania, the Easter Islanders or Pascuans have the most tragic history. The Europeans who came to the South Pacific were not a uniformly bad lot. But good or bad, it made little difference; they all brought their weapons, their religion and their diseases.

Easter Island first enters recorded history in 1722 when the Dutch admiral Jaakob Roggeveen aboard *The Arena* made a landfall at what he took to be "Davis Land." The landing was made on Easter Sunday and he named the place Paasch Eyland or Easter Island. The natives themselves did not seem to have any special name for their island. Why should they? To them it was the world. When Tahitians first came to the island in the 1870s they called it Rapa Nui, "Great Rapa," because it resembled Rapa Iti, an island they knew. Both names have stuck. It is Easter Island to the world at large and Rapa Nui to those who live there.

The behavior of the natives was astonishing and incomprehensible to the Dutch. They boarded the strange ship without any show of fear and clambered over it in high spirits. Suddenly they began stealing things and diving overboard with their prizes. The thefts were minor, sailors' caps (the Pascuans had a great fondness for caps), the Admiral's tablecloth and the like. The concept of private property was alien to the people of Easter Island, but the sailors did not understand. It made them suspicious and nervous.

When the first landing party went ashore the behavior of the throng assembled on the beach was even more bewildering and unnerving. Some of the natives were wildly friendly, others looked hostile and began throwing stones. As the landing party was advancing slowly, someone shouted, "Fire! Now's the moment!" Seconds later several natives lay dead on the beach; the rest had fled. Some sailor, perhaps frightened by the stones, had touched off the massacre. There was no evil design behind it, but the pattern had been set.

When the natives returned they were quiet and submissive. The men of *The Arena* seemed sorry for what they had done and presented the Islanders with flags as a token of respect. But they had little heart for a prolonged stay. In the brief encounter, however, the Dutchmen had caught sight of the colossal monuments, and they spent many hours on ship discussing them. They decided the "idols" were made of clay.

For half a century the island was forgotten. Then in 1770 a Spanish expedition still looking for the elusive "Davis Land" came to the island. The Spanish were shocked by what they considered the loose morals of the Pascuans. The women willingly offered themselves to the sailors, and the men of the island observed their activities with calm indifference. Ultimately the Spanish assumed the women's favors were being offered in payment for the trinkets the men were pilfering. The Spanish also claimed the island for the Kingdom of Spain and renamed it San Carlos. The natives obligingly made their marks on the deed of annexation and the Spanish sailed away.

Four years later the celebrated Captain Cook came to Easter

Island. To him the natives seemed in a wretched condition, a far worse state than earlier accounts indicated. Still the islanders were in high spirits. They sold Cook's men baskets of potatoes that were weighted with stones, then stole the potatoes back and resold them.

Other expeditions visited the island in the next few years, and in general the navigators retained the traditions of humanity and scientific inquisitiveness that marked the best of the explorers of the eighteenth century. But that era was drawing to a close. In 1808 the American ship *Nancy* carried off twenty-two Pascuans after a bloody battle. They hoped to sell them as slaves, but the natives escaped and drowned in a futile attempt to swim back home.

The year 1862 brought total disaster for Easter Island. In 1859 Chile began exploiting the guano deposits on islands off its coasts. It was an extremely profitable undertaking for the owners, but for those forced to labor on the blazing islands it was a death sentence. Death could come from several causes— overwork, starvation or disease. No one willingly would take on such a job. To combat the labor shortage a new breed of South American slave traders grew up. On December 12, 1862, a flotilla of Peruvian slavers anchored off the coast of Easter Island. All the horrors of the slave raids in black Africa were reenacted. A thousand captives were taken, including King Kamakoi and his son Maurata.

After a few months of forced labor for the guano companies, about a hundred remained alive. Finally the Bishop of Tahiti, backed by the French and British governments, urged the Peruvians to return the survivors to Easter Island. Most of them died on the return voyage. Only fifteen of the original thousand ever saw their home again, and for those who escaped the slavers it would have been better if these fifteen too had died, for they carried the germs of smallpox. Within months an epidemic was raging. For all practical purposes the religious and social system of Easter Island had been destroyed. The population which had once been in the thousands had fallen to a few hundred.

In 1864 Brother Eugène Eyard, a French missionary with a burning desire to convert the Pascuans, arrived on Easter Island. Brother Eugène was a good man who endured great hardships for his religion. He is still kindly remembered today. But his task was made much easier because the Pascuans' link with their own religious heritage had been severed. Most of the chiefs and priests were dead, and there was no effective group to oppose the new religion. When Brother Eugène died in August 1868 his final words were, "Are they all baptized?" They all had been.

Another Frenchman, Dutroux-Bornier, had less noble motives. He settled on the island in the hopes of converting it into a private estate. He surrounded himself with a bodyguard of armed natives and through trickery or force managed to acquire a large part of the land. The situation became so intolerable that the Bishop of Tahiti ordered his missionaries and their flock to leave the island. Three hundred did so, and the entire island would have been deserted if Dutroux-Bornier had not arranged that one hundred and eleven natives be left behind against their will. Ultimately Dutroux-Bornier committed one outrage too many and the natives murdered him.

Chile annexed the island in 1888 and leased it to the British firm of Williamson, Balfour and Company. The island was administered by Scotsmen, who herded all the natives into a single village and turned the rest of the island over to sheep. Still, it was better than what had gone before, and the

Pascuans prospered after a fashion. From a mere 111 in 1884, there are now nearly a thousand of them today.

In 1954 the government of Chile finally decided that the natives of their distant possession had some rights after all. They refused to renew the British company's lease and began to operate the sheep ranch for the benefit of the Pascuans.

With affluent Americans and others ranging farther and farther afield to find untouched and exotic vacation spots, Easter Island with its mysterious and romantic past has become something of a tourist attraction.

The coming of the white man was a disaster, but it would be wrong to believe that the people of Easter Island had lived in some sort of glorious "state of nature." The idea of the "noble savage" was current among educated Europeans of the eighteenth century. Many of the romantics who filled the ranks of the great travelers and explorers of that era saw reflections of the "noble savage" in the customs of peoples of distant lands.

But Easter Island society was not simple or "natural." It was highly structured. It had its kings and its slaves, its tribes and clans and the whole intricate rigidly observed system of social relationships and behavior commonly found in so-called "primitive" societies. To believe, as many of the early visitors did, that the Pascuans are just "grown-up children" makes it impossible to understand how they built the monuments which still astonish us.

The most unpleasant truth which shatters the illusion of the children of nature is that the Pascuans were cannibals. Every battle, and battles were frequent, ended with captives being tortured or eaten. Many traditional battle legends end the same way: ". . . They were cut in pieces. The vanquished, seized with panic, took refuge in caverns, where the victors sought them out. The men, women and children who were captured were eaten."

Cannibalism was a religious act, but simple revenge for outrages committed on kinsmen in the past seems to have been a more forceful motive. Then cannibalism was probably popular simply because the Pascuans liked to eat human flesh. "After all," notes one observer, "man was the only large mammal whose flesh was available."

Although cannibalism was an accepted part of the society, it was also a great crime and terrible insult. The result of each feast was an orgy of even more violent reprisals. Charming, friendly and likable, as they often seemed, the Easter Islanders were quickly roused to a state of rage. But we have no right to feel too smug in our civilized superiority. The same sort of boundless cruelty can be found lovingly described in early medievel epics, and echoes of cannibalism can be detected in European fairy tales.

If the Pascuans were just a cannibal society, they would merely provide an additional grisly footnote to the history of man, but they were a good deal more for they have left behind some really extraordinary accomplishments. Most obviously they built the great statues.

There is no mystery about how the statues were built. The two hundred or so unfinished monuments in the quarry on Rano Raraku give an excellent picture of how the sculptors worked. Almost all the statues were carved out of the volcanic rock with simple stone tools. The large number of statues left unfinished indicates that the sculptors mass-produced these giants, but they were not very inventive. The statues all were built on a single prototype, with only minor variations.

A more interesting problem is how the statues were moved and set up. Admiral Roggeveen looked at them and wondered.

"These stone figures filled us with amazement," he wrote, "for we could not understand how people without solid spars and without ropes were able to raise them . . ."

As late as 1948 one investigator declared that the stones could not possibly have been moved by men, but that they were transported by periodic volcanic eruptions.

An even more fantastic idea was recorded in 1933 by the myth collector Lewis Spence: "There is a tradition in the island of the former existence of an aerial gravitational tramway from the top of an eminence down to a great platform nearly a mile off, on the coast, and another from the same height reaching to a spot nearly two miles distant. On the ridge of the height are circular holes drilled deep in the rock, and into these, says tradition, were wedged high circular beams from the top of which huge ropes were stretched. By means of these the statues on their sledges were passed by gravitation to the site where they were to be erected."

The probable method is much less exotic. The anthropologist-adventurer Thor Heyerdahl, who proposed some quite exotic theories about the origins of Easter Island civilization, was very practical in his approach to discovering how the statutes were moved. He organized a crew of 180 Easter Islanders and they succeeded in dragging a 12-ton statue a considerable distance. A crew of 11 raised a fallen 25-ton statue in 8 days by levering it gradually and building up a blocking of small stones underneath it. When Heyerdahl asked the leader of the crew why so many people had puzzled over the movement of the statues, he was told it was because "No one ever asked *me.*"

There is nothing unique about transporting the Easter Island statues. Many people with primitive technologies have been able to move far heavier stones over longer distances.

The purpose of these statues has excited much wild speculation. Harold T. Wilkins, one of the searchers after lost continents, has a typical attitude: "The menacing stare of these cold-lipped, stern-eyed colossi of the cliff platforms must have played some mysterious, if not sinister part in whatever queer or occult rites, or ancestor-cults were celebrated in this island graveyard."

The basic purpose of the statues was discovered in 1914 by Mrs. Scoresby Routledge, who led the first scientific expedition to the island. She found that most of the statues were placed alongside burial enclosures. "In Easter Island the problem of the disposal of the dead was solved by neither earth-burial nor cremation, but by means of the omnipresent stones which were built up to make a last resting place for the departed. Such burial places are known as *ahu* . . ."

When Mrs. Routledge came to the island, some of the older residents could remember a time when the *ahu* were still used. The corpse was wrapped up and set on a platform and for several years the *ahu* district was taboo. Anyone who broke the taboo was likely to be brained by relatives of the dead man. After the mourning period, what was left of the body in the *ahu* was collected and buried, and there was a great feast.

Between 1722 and 1864 all of the *ahu* statues had been toppled. The statues most commonly seen in photographs are those on the slopes of Rano Raraku itself. Their purpose is less clear. There are some distinct stylistic differences between the *ahu* statues and those on the volcano slope, indicating that they may have been constructed during different periods. The *ahu* statues were always crowned by cylindrical "hats" of red volcanic rock. These "hats" most probably represented the topknot of hair traditionally worn by men of the island. The

Rano Raraku statues have no "hats." The *ahu* statues have fully sculpted eyes while the volcano statues lack distinct eyes. While the *ahu* statues have distinct bases so they could be set up on the stone platforms, the base of the volcano statues is a tapering peg, which was stuck into the soft soil of the slope. Some believe that the volcano statues are simply unfinished *ahu* statues.

The people of Easter Island obviously went through a period of frantic statue building. Then, apparently quite suddenly, the frenzy for construction ended and a frenzy of destruction began. The quarry with its hundred unfinished giants was abandoned. Metraux describes the scene:

"To the visitor walking round the quarry it seems as though this were a day of rest. The workmen have gone home to their villages but tomorrow they will be back . . . How could they fail to come back, these sculptors who have left their tools lying at the foot of the work, where one only has to bend down to pick them up?"

When Roggeveen landed in 1722, the *ahu* were still standing, but when the missionaries landed in 1864, not a single one was upright. Something drastic had happened, but what?

The people of Easter Island have a story: The woman who cooked for the sculptors was also sorceress. One day fishermen brought in a giant crayfish for a feast. The woman began cooking the crayfish with potatoes "which are good to eat with crayfish" but before it was finished she went away to see her brother. The sculptors opened the oven and ate the whole crayfish before the old woman returned. When she came back and found there was nothing left for her she was furious. "The old woman recited a spell. She said: 'Statues that are upright—fall down! It is the fault of the great crayfish, of the crayfish with the long tail of which you left nothing for me.

54

Never again shall you steal my food. Statues, remain still for ever.' All the statues fell, for the sorceress' bosom was full of anger."

Seekers for lost continents, and the cataclysms which caused them to disappear have been no less imaginative in explaining the mystery of the fallen statues. Witness this quote from Harold T. Wilkins: "One day, while the slaves and slave-artisans, under the eyes of their taskmasters, were putting the finishing touches to a number of great figures lying in a vast quarry-crater of a workship . . . a black cloud seemed suddenly to cover the face of the sun . . . The ground heaved violently in tremendous tremors . . . Mountainous waves of an ocean infuriated and maddened by some tremendous force swept right over the tall cliffs and crashed on the feet of the colossal images . . . May be mephitic gases overtook them [the workmen] on their way to shelter in the secret caves of the cliffs on that dreadful island . . . the mighty Pacific island-continent of Rutas-Mu-Gondwanaland had toppled her foundations deep, deep down into the hell of the abyss . . ."

There must be something deeply satisfying about catastrophes, for men have sought them so avidly. Even if one does not wish to accept the geological judgment that no continent ever sank in the mid-Pacific, and that Easter Island itself has been subject to no great catastrophe since its violent volcanic birth several millennia ago, the catastrophic explanation for the fallen statues would be hard to swallow. It would have to have taken place between 1722 and 1864, a time when European ships were arriving more or less regularly. Yet not a single explorer found any evidence of such a disaster.

The modern Easter Islanders can pluck from the shattered memories of their former culture a foggy and incomplete story of what really happened to the statues. During the end of the eighteenth and the beginning of the nineteenth century the island was wracked by an unusually fierce series of inter-tribal wars. One outrage triggered retribution, and so on. Perhaps the greatest insult that could be committed upon an enemy tribe would be to destroy the bodies of its honored dead and desecrate the sacred *ahus*.

The overthrowing of the statues did not happen in a single day or even a single year. Members of the Comte de La Pérouse's expedition of 1786 could be sketched in the shadow of a giant statue, but they noted that statues on another part of the island had been tipped over. By 1815 some of the statues La Perouse's men had seen intact were found fallen. In 1837 Admiral Dupetit-Thouars saw, as he sailed past, "a platform on which were set four red statues." But the missionaries who landed in 1864 found not a single standing statue, except those on the side of the volcano. These were not connected with any particular tribe so there was no reason to desecrate them. One wonders, incidentally, how the catastrophists explain why the great earth convulsions spared this set of statues.

Some very old men told scientists that in the time of their fathers the island was filled with the crash of falling statues. They called the conflicts "the wars of the throwing down of the statues."

Many of the "mysteries" of Easter Island that have for so long hypnotized the world are really not mysteries at all. But this does not mean that there are still not mysterious or un-explained things about the island. Foremost are the "talking boards."

Shortly after the natives had been converted to Christianity they sent the Bishop of Tahiti a long cord braided from their own hair as a gift. The cord was wound around what looked like an ordinary piece of wood. But when the bishop looked at the board closely he found that lines of little figures were cut into the wood. They did not look like ordinary decoration but rather like some sort of picture writing.

These engraved boards had been noticed earlier, but nobody, including the natives themselves, seemed to think they were particularly important. Before special notice was taken of them most of the boards, which once must have been quite numerous, were destroyed. Today only a handful of boards and a few other inscribed objects with the signs on them remain.

If the boards did actually contain a hieroglyphic system of writing, then deciphering it might throw a great deal of light on the history of Easter Island. Even if the boards merely contained ritual chants their very existence would be of paramount importance, because no other South Pacific island people possessed a written language. But no one knew how to decipher the writing, or could even be sure that it was writing at all.

According to tradition knowledge of the tablets was limited to an elite class of chanters or reciters called *tangata rongorongo*. Children of noble families were inducted into this class and underwent a long education in reading the tablets. Every year wars on the island were suspended for a great feast in which the best of the *tangata rongorongo* competed in reading the hymns written on the boards. It was like an ancient Greek dramatic competition. Good recitations were greeted with cheers, but the attentive audience hooted and ridiculed any errors they detected.

The slave raid of 1862 and the disasters that followed virtually wiped out the aristocratic classes of Easter Island, and by the time white men took an interest in the "talking boards" there was no one left who could read them. Several natives claimed they could. When they were brought together in a group, however, disagreement about the meaning of the symbols broke out.

Other attempts were equally unpromising. The same native would give a different reading of the same board on different days. One of the natives claimed he could read the boards. However, since he had become a good Catholic he was prevented from doing so because this represented a relapse to paganism. He did agree to read photographs of some of the boards. The recitation began well enough. Soon, however, the observers were disconcerted to realize that their reader didn't seem to be paying any attention to the number of symbols on each line, and he didn't even seem to notice when one photograph was replaced by another. The poor fellow was summarily dismissed as a fraud.

In 1932 the Hungarian linguist Wilhelm von Hevesy found what he believed to be significant similarities between the symbols on the Easter Island tablets and symbols used by the peoples of the ancient cities of the Indus valley. This identification simply deepened the mystery, because the Indus Valley scripts are also undeciphered. Besides, the two cultures are separated by thousands of miles and thousands of years. The Indus valley civilization is one of the oldest known, having flourished some five thousand years ago; the Easter Island scripts were still presumably being read a little over a hundred years ago. And how was knowledge of this script conveyed from the Indian subcontinent to a tiny patch of volcanic island in the middle of the Pacific, without leaving the slightest trace of its passage in the lands between? Finally, aside from the scripts there is not the vaguest resemblance between the orderly high civilization of the Indus and the primitive life of the Pascuans.

Other scholars believed they found a link between the Easter Island *rongorongo* boards and very early Chinese scripts. The distance and time are not so great, but then neither is the resemblance. In the 1950s a German scholar announced that he had partially deciphered the scripts, and surmised that peoples of other Pacific islands had used a similar form of writing but abandoned it long before the coming of the white man.

In 1938 the Viennese scholar Robert von Heine-Geldren had theorized that once there must have existed in Asia a form of writing that was parent both to Indus and to Chinese, and that it was spread to Easter Island by the migrations of the peoples from Asia to the Pacific islands.

Most scholars today believe that the Easter Island scripts were not a system of writing, in the strict sense of the term. Rather that they were "mnemonic" or memory-jogging devices. The symbols conveyed certain key elements in the story or chant, but the real skill of the *rongorongo* reader was his memory, and his interpretation of the symbols. If this is the case, the boards can never really be read by anyone who does not already know the tale they are trying to convey.

The controversy about the possible spread of the scripts from India to Easter Island brings up the final and most hotly debated question about the island: Who are the people and where did they come from?

Most authorities believe that Easter Islanders are Polynesians, a people who originally dwelt on the southeastern coast of Asia. During the second millennium B.C. the Chinese Empire was in a period of rapid expansion. The advancing Chinese pushed surrounding peoples outward, these in turn pushed their neighbors, and so on, until the Polynesians began to feel the pressure. They lived on the seashore and, having nowhere else to run, they took to the sea. During a century's long odyssey these wanderers populated islands over an enormous area of the Pacific. Their exact route and the dates they reached various islands are at present unknown, but until recently it has been assumed that they came to Easter Island late in the first millennium A.D.

The idea that the Easter Islanders came from Asia has been dramatically challenged in recent years by the attractive anthropologist-adventurer Thor Heyerdahl of Norway. Heyerdahl believes that the culture of the Easter Islanders, indeed of all the Polynesian peoples, originally came from the West, from South America.

This is shocking to conservative anthropologists and archaeologists, but the rest of his theory leaves them incredulous and more than a little angry. "Heyerdahl is actually convinced," writes Metraux, "that a people, or more exactly a group of men, with fair skin, aquiline noses and bushy beards exercised a decisive influence on the development of the American civilizations and in particular on those that flourished in the Andes, in ancient Peru. It was these mysterious civilizers who, having already assumed the white man's burden, set out on rafts in quest of new lands, once their mission had been accomplished in Peru."

There exists throughout the widely scattered pre-Columbian civilizations of Central and South America a cycle of rather vague legends of a fair-skinned, bearded god who came among the Indians, bringing them the fruits of civilization, and then vanished. The Aztecs and Toltecs called him Quetzalcoatl; to the Mayans he was Kukulcan, and among the Incas, Viracocha, or, according to Heyerdahl, Kon Tiki Viracocha.

Heyerdahl, of course, was not the first to notice these legends. In the past they have been used to prove that the

Romans, Phoenicians, Irish, Portuguese or people (always white) from the lost continents of Atlantis, Lemuria, or Mu had been the real force behind the great Indian civilizations. The legends were collected by white men, who were quite anxious to prove that only people of their own race could be civilized. Most of the theories were blatantly racist, and wildly illogical. Heyerdahl, however, can in no way be classed with the crew of crackpots that preceded him. He is a careful scientist who had done a great deal of important work among the American Indians and Polynesians.

In 1947 Heyerdahl set out to demonstrate part of his theory. With five companions he sailed a small Inca-style balsa raft, christened *Kon Tiki,* from the coast of Peru westward to the little Polynesian atoll of Raroia in the Tuamotus. The trip of 4300 nautical miles took 101 days; the power was the prevailing trade winds and ocean currents. The great adventure, which many had said was impossible, made Heyerdahl a celebrity. But his scientific colleagues did not immediately flock to his standard. To show that South American Indians could have sailed to Polynesia was one thing. Perhaps they had, but occasional contacts between South America and the islands did not prove that white men from Peru—or anyone from Peru—provided the basic spark for the Polynesian culture.

A few years later Heyerdahl led an archaeological expedition to Easter Island to look for more evidence in support of his theory. In addition to having the most spectacular ruins of any of the Polynesian islands, Easter Island had a geographical position that made it extremely important to Heyerdahl's theory. Of the countless islands of Polynesia, Easter is the farthest from Asia and the closest to South America. If the Polynesians came from Asia, they would have reached it last;

if they had migrated in the other direction, it would have been among the first colonized. Using radiocarbon dating tests Heyerdahl found evidence of human habitation on Easter Island in A.D. 380 (plus or minus one hundred years). This was far earlier than anyone except Heyerdahl himself would have placed the colonization of the island.

Heyerdahl's excavations did not reveal clear evidence of a simple migration from the Western Hemisphere. In order to fit in everything he found he had to construct three separate waves of migration. The first came about A.D. 380 and established the basic Easter Island civilization. These people, he believes, came directly from Peru and carried with them the skills of working stone. They constructed walls similar to those marvelous masonry works found in ancient Peru.

For an unknown reason this first civilization collapsed about 1100, and the island was in decline for many years until a new wave of immigrants arrived, also from Peru. This middle period saw the construction of the *ahus* with their stone giants.

Then about 1400, while the statue-building culture was at its peak, the real Polynesians began filtering in from the direction of Asia. "Nothing was found," Heyerdahl wrote, "to contradict the general opinion that the ancestors of the present population reached Easter Island extremely late. What we found was that another people was there to receive them."

According to Heyerdahl, even the Polynesian invaders themselves may not have come originally from Asia—they too may have started in Peru. "A combination of all known facts makes it possible that the present Polynesian stock, including the third-epoch Easter Islanders, reached their present area from eastern Asia after a long sojourn on the islands of the Northwest American coast, where the Japan Current sweeps the shore line with water from the Philippine Sea."

At first the newcomers were received peacefully, Heyerdahl believes, but finally warfare broke out between them and the statue builders. In Easter Island tradition, the wars that did so much to shatter their civilization are spoken of as a conflict between the short ears and the long ears. Heyerdahl identifies the short ears as the new immigrants and the long ears as the statue builders. The name long ears comes from the practice of some of the islanders of piercing and stretching their ear lobes in order to accommodate enormous ornamental plugs. Admiral Roggeveen had been impressed by the islanders exotic ears, and the statues all have unnaturally large lobes.

Tradition has it that the short ears ultimately won the battles and nearly exterminated (and probably consumed) the long ears. The statues were pulled down, and the unique Easter Island civilization was finished forever. Heyerdahl triumphantly points out that the Incas and other Peruvian Indians also deformed the lobes of their ears.

The Norwegian anthropologist leans heavily on the story of Hota Matu'a, the legendary discover of Easter Island and culture hero of the people. Hotu Matu'a was an ancient chief who was forced to leave his native land, "a group of islands toward the rising sun." With his followers he came to Easter Island, bringing with him all the edible plants and animals found on the island, the "talking boards" and all the other elements of Easter Island's unique civilization.

Ever since Heyerdahl proposed his theory critics have been taking shots at it. Heyerdahl's use of the island's legends opens him to particularly severe attack. The story of Hotu Matu'a, for example, is based on a version related not by a native but by Alexander P. Salmon, a Tahitian who settled on the island in 1877. Whereas this informant told one inquirer that Hotu Matu'a sailed eastward, he told other visitors Hotu Matu'a had come from the opposite direction. The Easter Islanders and Peruvians deformed their ear lobes, but so do the peoples of some of the Polynesian islands closer to Asia. The stone-working techniques of Easter Island and Peru bear only a superficial resemblance to one another, say the critics. The Easter Islanders used thin slabs of stone to face coarse rubble walls, while the Peruvians used solid blocks of stone. Heyerdahl says the Easter Island script was brought from South America and has even identified some South American animals among the figures, but the South American Indians had no written language.

Writes Metraux: "What surprises me is that Easter Island culture does not present more analogies with the various civilizations of ancient Peru, . . . I have often wondered why the Peruvian Indians did not preserve in the Pacific the two arts in which they excelled—pottery and weaving."

Despite all the publicity, Heyerdahl has not won the day. He strikes one as a man with an *idée fixe*. From 1937 to the present he has pursued this idea, with great courage and great ingenuity, but he is too quick to pull from the confusion that surrounds the origins of Easter Island culture those facts that seem to support his theory, and to ignore those that do not.

Perhaps future expeditions will clear the picture. More likely, though, nothing will ever completely dispel the aura of mystery that surrounds Easter Island. For the real mystery is not where the people came from, or how they dragged their statues around. It lies in the psychology of these people who seemed to live such an extravagant life under circumstances of almost unbelievable isolation.

FOUR

STONEHENGE

The Sunrise Circle

On Salisbury Plain in the pastoral southern English county of Wiltshire is the monument called Stonehenge. It is a circle of enormous stones and it is very old. By the time recorded history caught up with Stonehenge, people had already forgotten who built it or why. Certainly the Romans didn't know, and they didn't care very much. After their conquest of Britain in the early years of the Christian era, their writers hardly mention Stonehenge. Why should they? The Romans who had conquered Egypt with her pyramids and inconceivably ancient civilization were not going to be impressed by a circle of stones. They may have even made a few half-hearted attempts to destroy the old monument, fearing that it would become a gathering place for anti-Roman, nationalist revolutionaries. But Stonehenge survived the Romans.

When the Romans withdrew, the natives of the British Isles lost much of their contact with the great world outside. They were forced to turn their energy and imagination toward their own land. In the dark ages which followed the Roman withdrawal, and the invasions of the Saxons and other barbarians, the people of Britain first began to try to account for Stonehenge. Documents from the dark ages are scarce, and the earliest written accounts of Stonehenge are lost. But there must have been a great deal of popular speculation about the monument, for by the twelfth century it had become firmly embedded in the complex legendary history that the people of the British Isles were fabricating for themselves.

In the twelfth century we first run across the name Stonehenge. It's a strange name, and we don't know who first used it, or why. The historian Henry of Huntingdon says that the word means "hanging stones" and that it is a good name because the stones seem to "hang as it were in the air," probably a reference to the lintels perched atop the great uprights. This is the feature of Stonehenge that first strikes the modern visitor, and there were more uprights and lintels in place in Henry's day than in our own.

Others have attempted to explain the name by saying that the stones of the monument were a place from which condemned criminals were hung. There is no evidence this was ever done. Stonehenge seems always to inspire morbid fantasies and bloody associations.

The greatest myth collector and compiler of the twelfth century was Geoffrey of Monmouth. Geoffrey's work, *History of the Kings of Britain*, contains the information on which all the later stories of King Arthur are based. Stonehenge is part of the story. It is pictured as a monument to Briton warriors, treacherously slain on Salisbury Plain by the invading Saxons.

According to Geoffrey, the king of the Britons Ambrosius Aurelianus visited the spot in Salisbury where "earls and princes lay buried" and was so moved by the scene that he determined to build a monument. He turned for aid to the wizard Merlin.

Geoffrey is describing a time some six or seven centuries before his own. The Romans have recently withdrawn and the native Britons, who have thoroughly adopted the Roman mode of life, have been abandoned to face barbaric invaders, most notably the Saxons.

The former Roman subjects put up a stubborn, if ultimately unsuccessful, defense of their island. There is evidence that one of their leaders was Ambrosius Aurelianus, a man either of Roman descent or from a native family that had adopted a Roman name. Geoffrey makes Ambrosius the brother of Uther Pendragon, whom most legends name as the father of King Arthur. As is typical of this kind of legendary material, the more threads you try to unravel the more tangled the skein becomes.

What we have here is an example of the popular tendency to ascribe all sorts of great deeds to a known popular hero. So the crafty Merlin got credit for constructing or at least moving Stonehenge. Merlin made this suggestion to Ambrosius:

"If thou be fain to grace the burial-place of these men with a work that shall endure forever, send for the Dance of the Giants that is in Killaraus, a mountain in Ireland. For a structure of stones is there that none of this age could raise save his wit were strong enough to carry his art. For the stones be big, nor is there stone anywhere of more virtue, and, so they be set up round this plot in a circle, even as they be now set up, here shall they stand for ever."

Geoffrey adds a few more details. "The Giants of old" had carried the stones to Ireland "from the furthest ends of Africa." Africa was the traditional source of all wondrous things. The stones seemed to have magical healing powers and this is why the Giants wanted them. Geoffrey is obviously referring to another legend, known in his own time but lost in ours.

The king's brother Uther was put in charge of an army of fifteen thousand men and went to Ireland to steal the Giants' Dance. The Irish tried to protect their national treasure but were defeated. However, the task of moving the stones was too much for Uther's army. They tried all the conventional transporting devices of the time, but to no avail. Finally the useful Merlin had to be called in. He "put together his own engines," which in some unspecified manner made it easy to move the stones to the ships and sail them to England. This feat, notes Geoffrey, "proved yet once again how skill surpasseth strength."

There is another possible connection between Merlin and Stonehenge. Some scholars believe that the name "Merlin" is taken from "Myrddin," the name of an ancient Celtic sky god, who may have been worshiped at open stone monuments like Stonehenge.

The idea that Merlin had put Stonehenge on Salisbury Plain took firm hold in the public mind and dominated most of the thinking about the monument for centuries. But by the fifteenth century skeptics had appeared, and scholars began casting about to find someone to replace Merlin. The Elizabethan historian and antiquary William Camden rejected the Giants' Dance idea as absurd. "For mine own part, about these points [a dispute over how Stonehenge was built] I am not curiously to argue and dispute, but rather to lament with much griefe that the Authors of so notable a monument are thus buried in oblivion." Camden then went on to speculate that the stones were not natural, "but artifically made of pure sand, and by some glewie and unctuous matter knit and in-corporate together . . ." This is an attitude that crops up again and again about Stonehenge. When confronted with those enormous stones, it is very difficult to believe they could have been moved by ordinary means.

Organized investigation of Stonehenge began in the seven-teenth century. In the early years of that century King James I sent the great architect Inigo Jones to examine this most an-cient relic in his realm. Jones was impressed and, being a thoroughly civilized man himself, decided that no "savage and barbarous people, knowing no use at all of garments," could have built Stonehenge. So much for the ancient Britons. Jones rejected "that ridiculous fable, of Merlin's transporting the stones out of Ireland," as "an idle conceit." He also spiked the idea that the Druids had built Stonehenge. "I find no mention, that they were at any time either studious in archi-tecture, (which in this subject is chiefly to be respected) or skilful in anything else conducting thereunto. For, Academies of Design were unknown to them: publique Lectures in Mathematiques not read amongst them: . . ." As we shall see, later scholars felt quite differently about the Druids.

To the civilized architect only a people capable of pro-ducing civilized architects like himself would be capable of building Stonehenge. There was only one candidate—the Romans. Inigo Jones declared that Stonehenge was a Roman temple. His approach to Stonehenge was light-hearted. He wasn't at all disturbed that none of the copious Roman records contained a word about the construction of Stonehenge, or that Stonehenge did not resemble any Roman temple. Inigo Jones had presented his theory—incomplete as it was—but he had no intention of being dogmatic about it.

"Whether, in this adventure, I have wafted my Barque into

the wished Port of Truths discovery concerning Stoneheng, I leave to the judgment of Skilfull Pilots."

Jones's theories were published in 1655, three years after his death. Because of his great reputation the Roman idea gained wide acceptance. But it did not smother other theories. The royal physician to Charles II, Dr. Walter Charleton, put forth the idea that the monument had been built by the Danes, "when they had this nation in subjection," as a royal court or place of coronation for their kings. Edmund Bolton said it had been constructed on the orders of the fabled British queen Boadicea, who had led an early revolt against the Romans. Others ascribed it to a number of other real or imaginary early British monarchs.

Round and round the controversy went, and all the time Stonehenge was becoming more famous, and drawing to Salisbury Plain a flock of tourists which continues to this day. The diarist Samuel Pepys visited the site in 1668, and wrote on June 11 of that year, "God knows what their [the stones] use was!"

Up to this point most of the theorizing about Stonehenge had been based on secondhand information, or at best, a cursory examination of the monument. It is ironic that the first man to make a thorough study of Stonehenge was a person known for his inattentiveness to truth and detail. John Aubrey was characterized by his enemies as "roving and magotieheaded" and Aubrey himself admitted that he "wanted patience to go through Knotty Studies."

But Aubrey had advantages as an investigator. He was highly intelligent and an excellent observer. He was also a dedicated antiquary, one of that group of embryonic archaeologists who did so much to stimulate man's interest in the past. In addition, he had been born quite near Stonehenge and knew the monument and surrounding area well. Around 1650 Aubrey began his investigation of Stonehenge. He made many observations which had escaped earlier visitors, and he probably contributed more to the study of Stonehenge than any other single individual. He also did the monument one great disservice—he said that it had been built by the Druids.

Aubrey did not originate the Druid-Stonehenge idea. It was popular enough in the 1620s for Inigo Jones to emphatically reject it. But bolstered by Aubrey's prestige, the Druid idea got a new lease on life. Even Aubrey was unsure of his identification and confessed he was "gropeing in the Dark." Sixty years later William Stukeley took up the cause of the Druids with a passion.

Stukeley was a British eccentric in the grand tradition. A surgeon of great reputation and intimate friend of such notables as Sir Isaac Newton, he was also a frenzied nationalist and religious oddball. Late in life he entered holy orders and became obsessed with the mission of reconciling Christianity with the "aboriginal patriarchal religion" of the Druids. So vigorous was his defense of the Druids that he became known as "The Arch-Druid."

Stukeley's surveys of the Stonehenge area are a mixture of useful observation and nonsense. He sent the Druid idea careening wildly into the realm of the occult. Over the next two centuries mystics tried to find associations between Stonehenge and the Great Pyramid. They searched Stonehenge for astrological associations and made the Druids the repositories of the "Ancient Wisdom of the East." For all its wrongheaded foolishness, perhaps because of it, Stukeley's Druid-Stonehenge crusade made a tremendous impact. Even today, most people have the vague notion that the Druids built Stonehenge.

On every midsummer's day a sad-funny little group of

white-robed cultists who claim to be the spiritual descendants of the ancient Druids gather in Stonehenge to greet the rising sun with their own version of a Druidic ritual.

After we peel away all the unjustified speculation about the Druids, we realize we really know very little about them. The Druids were the priests and judges of the Celtic peoples, and seem to have provided a sort of loose intertribal unity among warring tribes. They probably arrived in Britain from the mainland in about the fourth century B.C. Britain became the stronghold of Druidic influence, which extended throughout much of northern Europe.

Since the Druids had no written language we have no first-hand knowledge of their practices. Our picture is based on brief references to them made by classical writers, mostly Romans, who, it must be remembered, were busily conquering the Celtic peoples, and would not be likely to give this powerful Celtic priesthood a very favorable press. Julius Caesar encountered the Druids during his conquest of Gaul. Caesar also visited Britain, but made no mention of Druids there. Of a Druidic festival Caesar wrote:

"They have colossal images, the limbs of which, made of wicker-work, they fill with living men and set on fire; and the victims perish, encompassed by the flames. They regard it as acceptable to the gods to punish those who are caught in the commission of theft, robbery, or any other crime; but in default of criminals, they actually resort to the sacrifice of the innocent."

A century later Pliny, in his *Natural History*, describes the oak as the sacred tree of the Druids, and tells of their ritual of cutting mistletoe with a golden sickle. Another Roman, Diodorus Siculus, notes that the Druids made their prophecies by examination of the entrails of human sacrificial victims.

For the last few centuries Celtophyles have tried to white-wash the reputation of the Druids, but the evidence for their practice of human sacrifice is too strong to ignore. Human sacrifice was common among the primitive people of Europe. The earliest Romans engaged in practices very like those which they professed to abhor among the Celts.

The pagan Romans were tolerant of other religions. They persecuted the Druids because the priests inspired the Celts to resist Roman rule. When the Romans became Christian, they lost their tolerance for other religions, and continued the persecution because the Druids resisted Christianity. In the end, the Druids and Druidism were stamped out completely.

Isolated, mysterious, and just plain spooky, Stonehenge seems the perfect place for the sacrificial rituals of the Druids. The Druids may have used Stonehenge for some of their rituals, and they may even have conducted human sacrifices there. We have no evidence that they did not, although the scanty records indicate that their favorite places of worship were groves and other wooded places, quite unlike Stonehenge. But they certainly did not build Stonehenge, because the monument had been completed at least a thousand years before any Druid set foot in England.

So if it wasn't the Druids, the Romans, the Britons, (or the Saxons, Danes, Atlanteans or Phoenicians, other popular candidates for the ownership of Stonehenge) who built it? The answer provided by modern archaeology is simple, indisputable, and at first glance disappointing. Stonehenge was built by the prehistoric people, or rather by a series of prehistoric peoples, who inhabited southern England between 1800 B.C. and 1400 B.C.

The Roman conquest of Britain was so complete that virtually all the stories of the people who inhabited the land before the coming of the Romans have been lost. From Ireland and other unconquered areas there are odd and fragmentary tales of the early peoples—giants, conquerors from Greece, wizards, invaders from India, etc. The tales are a mixture of classical and Christian legend, just plain fairy stories, and perhaps a core of half-remembered history. But they are of little use in finding the builders of Stonehenge. We must rely almost entirely on archaeology.

The field of prehistoric archaeology has advanced tremendously over the last fifty years, and since the British retain a reverential attitude toward their own past, Britain has been one of the most minutely explored areas in the world from an archaeological point of view. From simple tools, bits of pottery and rude graves the archaeologist can construct a surprisingly good picture of the way men of the past lived. Still, without the legends the picture is flat. We don't know any of the great events, or heroes, we don't know what these people worshiped, or feared, we don't even know what they called themselves.

The first people we are concerned with in the building of Stonehenge are the Windmill Hill People, who inhabited Southern England in about 2400 B.C. Archaeologists have to call prehistoric people something so they usually take a name for a particular culture from the place where evidence of its existence was first found, or from some particular artifact associated with that culture. Windmill Hill is located quite near Stonehenge. The simple tools found there indicate that the Windmill Hill People were primitive farmers and herdsmen. The same sort of implements dating from earlier times have been found on the continent. The Windmill Hill People were probably migrants who settled among the native roving hunting bands.

About 2000 B.C. more migrants from the continent arrived. This group was probably not numerous, for the artifacts of the Windmill Hill People continue to predominate, but they are important for our story because these new people brought with them a love of impressive tombs. They placed their dead in tombs made from great stones, buried under long mounds of earth. Not that the Windmill Hill People were without building skills, but they were employed for more practical purposes. Atop Windmill Hill itself is a huge earthwork enclosure called a "causewayed camp" that probably served as a cattle pound.

The Windmill Hill People and the recent migrants merged and formed a new culture, which archaeologists label Secondary Neolithic. It was this mixed group that started building Stonehenge.

Stonehenge is generally thought of as a circle of giant stones, but it is a much more complex structure than that. When it began, it may have had only one stone in it, and even that has been disputed. Originally Stonehenge was two circular banks of earth separated by a ditch. The circle was a little over the length of a football field in diameter. The outer bank was about six feet wide and two or three feet high. The ditch itself was really nothing more than a series of quarry holes. The inner bank, when originally constructed, would have been quite impressive. It was some six feet high and twenty feet wide, and must have been bright white due to the chalky nature of the soil of Salisbury Plain.

The earthwork is broken on the northeast side by a broad entrance gap. From this entrance runs an ancient road called the Avenue, bounded by a bank and ditch on either side. The Avenue runs downhill for about two miles, until it meets the River Avon. In the center of the Avenue, not far outside of the main bank and ditch, is a huge, elongated boulder standing some fifteen feet high and weighing an estimated thirty-five tons. This is the Heel Stone, and it is surrounded by a bank and ditch of its own. Most, but not all, authorities believe that the Heel Stone was part of the first phase of Stonehenge construction. It is made of a kind of natural sandstone called sarsen. Boulders of this type can be found in Marlborough Downs some twenty miles north of Stonehenge.

The origins of the name Heel Stone are uncertain. There is a story that the devil had an argument with a monk and threw a huge stone at him, hitting the monk in the heel. The holy man was unhurt, but his heel left a mark in the stone. The problem is there is no heel-like mark in the stone, nor does it resemble a heel in any other way. Perhaps the name was originally applied to another stone, and over the years the description became confused, but the name has stuck. Some even spell it Hele Stone, to give the name a more antique flavor.

When John Aubrey investigated Stonehenge, he discovered a ring of fifty-six, irregularly shaped, but regularly spaced holes just inside the main bank. These were named after him. Modern archaeologists have found cremated human bones at the bottom of some of these holes, but they do not seem to have been regular graves. The Aubrey Holes were dug and filled in in ancient times. Careful investigation has indicated that they never held stones, wooden posts, or anything else, except the bones and some ornaments. They were just holes.

For many years it was thought the holes were dug for stones but that this particular arrangement was abandoned (there were many false starts in the construction of Stonehenge). Then in 1950 a fragment of cremated bone from one of the holes was radiocarbon dated at 1850 B.C., proving that the holes were part of the earliest phase of construction.

That is all there was to Stonehenge I, at least all that we know of it. There may have been a structure of wood or other perishable material inside, but not a trace has been found. Similar, though smaller, earthen circles, dating from about the same period, have been found in other parts of the British Isles and on the Continent. If the people who lived around Salisbury Plain had stopped at this point, the monument would make an interesting article for an archaeological journal, but it would hardly attract a quarter of a million visitors annually.

Stonehenge II was begun some hundred and fifty years after the first phase of construction was completed. Fragments of a particular type of pottery, called Beaker pottery, have been found in association with this part of the work. These fragments showed that the ubiquitous Beaker People had arrived at Salisbury Plain. The Beaker People are named after a particular type of finely worked drinking vessel which they made.

Fragments of Beaker pottery have been found all over the British Isles and on the Continent from Poland to Portugal. The Beaker People seem to have been a race of itinerant traders who moved in small groups over immense distances. Their chief item of barter was bronze, a material unknown to the Neolithic farmers among whom they moved. The Beaker People probably came originally from Spain, where they picked up their knowledge of metalworking from the advanced civilizations of the Mediterranean and Near East.

Along with the bronze they may have carried another item which would make them welcome wherever they went—beer.

That is why they needed all those beakers. The archaeologist Geoffrey Bibby gives this imaginary description of them:

"Whether the Beaker Folk were the inventors of beer we do not know, but it is an attractive thought that the last rite performed by the traveling merchants burying one of their number in foreign soil, far from his native Sierras, may well have been to fill up his tankard to the brim with ale and to place it ready to hand in the grave."

Only in England did the Beaker People seem to become the dominant part of the population. Examination of their remains show them to be racially different from the indigenous population.

These ambitious travelers decided to make some additions to the principal monument of their new homeland. They added the bluestone circle, in one way the most remarkable feature of Stonehenge. The bluestones (they are really five different types of rock, all of which have a bluish tint when wet) could only have come from one place, the Prescelly Mountains in Wales, 130 miles, as the crow flies, from Stonehenge. The bluestones are not the largest stones in the monument, but originally there must have been more than eighty of them, each weighing up to five tons. The easiest way to move these stones would have been by water, and the most direct route would have involved floating the stones on rafts over 215 miles of fairly safe waterways, then dragging or rolling them overland for about 25 miles. The transportation would have been a difficult and time-consuming task, but by no means an impossible or miraculous one.

The builders began construction of a double circle of bluestones in the center of the main circle. The upright stones were placed close together; it is possible that they were meant to be topped with crosspieces or lintels, so as to form a complete circle of arches. We do not know, for the circle was never completed, and there seems to have been some confusion as to what the placement of the stones was to be. The whole bluestone project was abandoned, or at least radically changed around 1500 B.C.

Archaeologists assign the building of the third and final stage of Stonehenge to the Wessex People. Wessex is just one of many names for the area in which Stonehenge is located, and the Wessex People are no new group, but rather a blending of the Beaker People and the earlier inhabitants. There had emerged among the Wessex People a class of what has been called "Bronze Age Merchant Princes." They carried on a metal trade with Ireland and Western Europe, and perhaps extended their influence even as far as the eastern Mediterranean. This trade made them enormously wealthy, by the standards of the time, as their elaborately furnished graves indicate. With wealth came the luxury of being able to set large numbers of men to a task which did not directly involve making a living. Practically every people seems to have the desire to express itself in some sort of monumental construction. Poor, primitive societies simply do not have the time to spare. For several hundred years, the people of southern Britain had been well off enough to allow some of their number to take time for the construction of the first stages of Stonehenge and other similar monuments. Now, with vastly increased wealth and leisure at their command, the Wessex merchants decided to make a really spectacular alteration in the monument of Salisbury Plain.

They sent their workmen back to Marlborough Downs—from whence the Heel Stone came—for more gigantic sarsen boulders. Eighty of them, weighing up to fifty tons each, were dragged the twenty miles to Stonehenge. Whereas in the past, stones of appropriate shape were chosen, and set up in their natural state, the workmen of the Wessex People carefully shaped and dressed the huge sarsens, so as to give Stonehenge a "finished" look, more typical of the civilizations of the Mediterranean than of the bronze age peoples of northern Europe. The bluestone circle was dismantled and in its place was set up a circle of thirty sarsen uprights joined across the top by lintels enclosing a horseshoe of five even larger sarsen trilithons (a freestanding, three-stone structure of two uprights capped by a lintel). It is the ruins of these enormous sandstone "gateways" that make up the most memorable part of what the modern visitor sees at Stonehenge. The largest standing trilithon is twenty-four feet high, including lintel, but the central trilithon of the horseshoe, which has now fallen, was even larger.

The builders still did not seem to be able to make up their minds what to do about the bluestones, which had been brought at such great cost all the way from Wales. First they set up what has been called the bluestone oval. This may have been a smaller replica of the horseshoe of great sarsen trilithons. But they didn't like that arrangement so they tore it down, and made a horseshoe of upright bluestones inside the sarsen horseshoe, and a full circle of upright bluestones between the sarsen horseshoe and the sarsen circle. The movement of the bluestones is hard to trace, since most of them have disappeared long ago, being chipped into nothingness by souvenir hunters with hammers or being carted away in pieces by farmers of an area which contains no natural rocks.

But with the final disposition of the bluestones, building at Stonehenge was at an end. The monument was as complete as it ever was to be about 1400 B.C. Building had been going on for at least four hundred years. We do not know why the

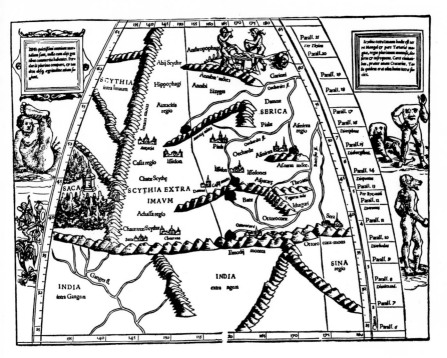

Medieval map shows grotesque creatures believed to inhabit distant lands.

The island of Atlantis as shown on a map drawn in 1678.

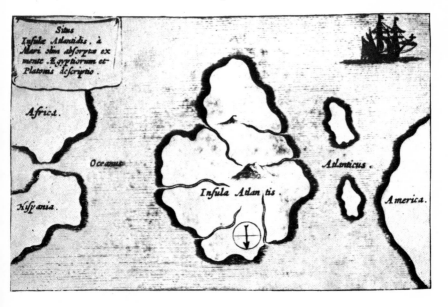

Statues on the slopes of the volcano Rano Raraku on Easter Island.

The Comte de La Pérouse's romantic vision of Easter Island and its people after his visit there in 1786. Note that the statues are still intact.

Easter Islanders entertain the crew of a visiting ship.

Stone tablets with Easter Island script.

Photo by Bridget Smith

Stonehenge, the most celebrated of all prehistoric monuments.

Axes inscribed in sarsen at Stonehenge.

Some of the stones of the Avebury monument.

Silbury Hill, the "Great Pyramid" of Europe.

Two views of King
Arthur and his knights
of the Round Table.

A romantic version of the death of Arthur. From a painting by Sir Joseph Noel Paton.

St. Michael's Chapel atop Glastonbury Tor, the highest point of the "Isle of Avalon."

Photo by Bruce Frisch

A comparison of Indus Valley script (left column) and Easter Island script (right column).

Indus Valley seal showing humped cattle.
The American Museum of Natural History

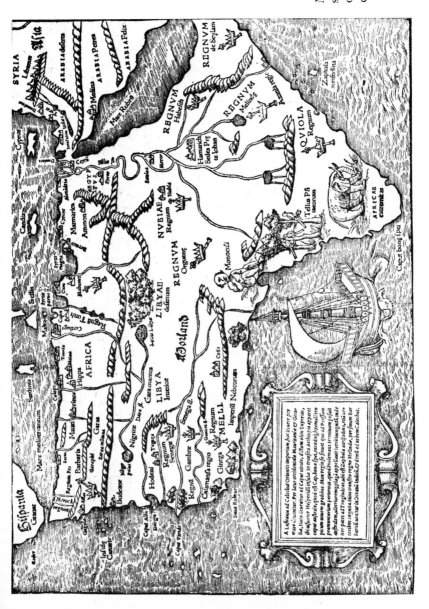

Medieval map of Africa showing the Kingdom of Prester John in the center of the continent.

Wall at Zimbabwe. Note the chevron design at the top.

Interior of Zimbabwe ruins.

A plaster reproduction of an Olmec head. The original was found at San Lorenzo, Mexico.

Drawing courtesy of Science Digest

Olmec "baby face" statuette.

Olmec "tiger face"
sculpture.

A recently discovered statuette of
an Olmec rain god.

Sir Walter Raleigh at Trinidad where he captured Antonio de Berrio.

builders decided they were finished, or how long they used Stonehenge after it was finished.

After we have discovered who built Stonehenge, the next natural question is, how was it built? To the modern visitor, who cannot imagine anything as large as the sarsen boulders being moved without cranes and bulldozers, it seems as though Stonehenge was built by Merlin's magical engine. The real answer is much less romantic, and surprisingly simple. The secret of the building of Stonehenge lay in the skillful use of simple tools and techniques, and a lavish expenditure of human time and human labor.

The original ditch and bank were dug from the hard chalk with picks made from the antlers of the red deer. (Many broken antlers have been found abandoned in the ditch.) The broken chalk rubble would then be hauled away in wicker baskets. It was hard work, but the antler pick was not as bad a tool as might be imagined. Modern tests have shown that a digger with a metal-headed pick can do only slightly better than one equipped with an antler pick. The entire ditch-bank arrangement of Stonehenge I could have been dug by a few hundred men in a single summer.

In 1954 British Broadcasting Corporation re-created the moving of the bluestones over land and water. Using concrete replicas of the bluestones, they constructed a pontoon raft for water transport. The B.B.C. investigators found that four men could easily control such a raft by means of poles in shallow water and that one man might have done so. In deeper water, they theorized sails or oars could have been used to help move the raft.

Land transport was considerably more difficult. After having teams of sturdy young men tug along at the concrete block, first when it was simply lashed to a sledge, and then when rollers were put under the sledge, the investigators decided that about sixteen men per ton would be needed to move the stones a mile or less a day.

The sarsens averaged thirty tons, and had to be moved more than twenty miles on land. Aside from the haulers, hundreds of extra men would have been needed to move the rollers, clear the brush, guide the sledge, provide food for the workmen, etc. It would have taken a thousand men at least seven years to get the sarsens to Stonehenge. Dressing and smoothing the sarsens would have cost another million man-hours of labor, according to one estimate.

With levers and ropes, two hundred men could have raised the uprights of the sarsen circle; perhaps an extra hundred would have been needed for the larger uprights of the sarsen trilithon horseshoe. Raising the lintels of twenty tons or so to the top of the uprights seems the most formidable task of all. We have no way of knowing exactly how it was done, but the best guess is that the lintels were raised a few feet at a time with levers. With each rise, a platform was built underneath the stone, until finally in slow stages it was brought to the level of the top of the uprights on a series of wooden platforms. Another possibility is that earth or wooden ramps were constructed alongside the uprights, so the lintels could be dragged up.

Totaling up all the work involved, Gerald Hawkins, a British-born astronomer, estimates a minimum of 1,500,000 man-days of physical labor, plus "an incalculable but certainly large amount of brainwork," must have been needed for this vast operation.

Fantastic? Not really. The Egyptians, the Incas, the Chinese and many other peoples of the past have put forth similar and even greater communal efforts. And Hawkins draws a comparison between the building of Stonehenge and the U.S. space program.

"The Space Program takes about one percent of our gross national product; Stonehenge must have taken at least a corresponding amount. Their building effort may have required more of them than our Space Program does of us; correspondingly, it could have meant much more to them."

Just what did Stonehenge mean to its builders? What did they use it for? Just about everybody who has ever theorized about Stonehenge has declared that it was a temple. This is a negative judgment. Stonehenge does not look like a castle or a fortress. It has no obvious practical use at all—so it must be a temple. Since there seemed no way of telling what sort of worship went on there, people began to invent things. Druidophiles saw in one of the stones a table on which the initiates of the order eviscerated their human victims with the golden sickle. They named the stone the Slaughter Stone. The name gives the tourist a delightful chill, but it's nonsense. When Stonehenge was originally built, the so-called Slaughter Stone stood upright. It could have served as a table only since it has fallen over, sometime within the last few hundred years. The same objection can be raised to the name Altar Stone. It too was an upright and it too has fallen over.

Since Stonehenge is roofless, most people have assumed that the worship there had something to do with the sky. In the latter part of the eighteenth century, observers first noticed that if one stood on the Altar Stone, which is about in the middle of Stonehenge, on the longest day of the year (June 21) and looked out toward the Avenue, he would see the sun rise above the Heel Stone. This idea has become so widely circulated that today's pseudo-Druids choose sunrise of June 21 as the day in which to hold their ceremonies at Stonehenge. As a matter of fact, the sun does not rise directly over the Heel Stone on June 21; it rises a bit to the left. The astronomer Sir Norman Lockyer recognized this in 1901, but he noted that the point at which the sun rises has changed slightly since Stonehenge was built. Sir Norman contended that the sun originally would have risen directly over the Heel Stone. Unfortunately, Sir Norman had calculated the wrong date for the construction of Stonehenge. So for a moment the theory was out. Then astronomers recalculated the point at which the sun would have risen about 1800 B.C. and found that it would have risen over the Heel Stone, so Sir Norman might have arrived at the right conclusion, by the wrong route.

But there are still difficulties. Over the centuries, the Heel Stone has tipped somewhat so we don't know exactly what its original position was. Then what does "rise directly over the Heel Stone" mean? Is it the moment when the first flash of morning light is seen, or is it when the entire orb of the sun is visible? Small points, perhaps, but extremely important if the purpose of Stonehenge was to determine the longest day of the year. Then where would the observer stand? He could not have stood, as popularly believed, on the Altar Stone, because the Altar Stone was an upright. Was there some special spot in the center of Stonehenge? None has ever been located, but then the center of the monument has never been excavated either. So even this seemingly simple solar alignment presents innumerable problems and unanswered questions.

From time to time various other astronomical uses have been ascribed to Stonehenge. In 1963 the astronomer Gerald Hawkins made a careful study of the monument and with the aid of a computer came to the conclusion that "each significant stone aligns with at least one other to point to some extreme position of the sun or moon." If such alignments really existed, they would have constituted an accurate way of determining the length of a year, an extremely important piece of knowledge for members of an agricultural society to have. I will not attempt to summarize Hawkins' mass of evidence here; anyone who wishes to pursue the subject further should read his admirable book *Stonehenge Decoded*.

More remarkable than the astronomical alignments was Hawkins' discovery that the mysterious Aubrey Holes could have been used as an eclipse predictor. For every prescientific people an eclipse is an awesome and terrifying event. Hawkins believes that the priests of Stonehenge could move a marker stone around the series of Aubrey Holes from year to year, and thus be able to determine the cycle of eclipses. This would not have had the practical significance of being able to calculate the length of the year, but it would have given the priests the tremendous power of being able to predict one of nature's most spectacular phenomena. It is not hard to imagine what an impression this knowledge would make on the ordinary people of the stone and bronze ages.

Hawkins' theories received a great deal of publicity; they were even the subject of an hour-long television show. In America the general impression is that Hawkins "solved" the problem of Stonehenge. True, some scholars think he has. Other astronomers, like Fred Hoyle of Cambridge, have even added their own astronomical ideas to the theory. But not everyone thinks Hawkins is right.

In Britain, where Stonehenge stands second only to the Crown as a national monument, the response has often been hostile. R. J. C. Atkinson, an archaeologist who spent years working at Stonehenge, described Hawkins' theories as "tendentious, arrogant, slipshod and unconvincing." This may be the ill-tempered growl of an old conservative who sees a young radical from a different field of study moving in on his territory, but Atkinson and others have made some telling points against Hawkins.

The basic contention of all the critics is that Hawkins has erected too grand a theory on scanty evidence. For example, for his ideas about the Aubrey Holes to work there would have to be fifty-six of them. There may be fifty-six, but no one knows for sure; others believe there may a few more, or less. Then Hawkins has a lot of numbers he can play with. The numbers game has been played with many monuments, particularly the Great Pyramid of Egypt where another astronomer, a century ago, found all sorts of significance, astronomical and otherwise, in its construction. Hawkins is far more scrupulous than the pyramidologists, but it is sobering to recall that the most astonishing conclusions can be reached if one wishes to play the numbers game diligently.

What bothers this writer most is that the design of Stonehenge was changed so many times over the centuries. Its use as a calendar would only have been possible during the final phase, and then the builders were not farmers, for whom the time of year would have been vital, but merchants, a group less concerned about the change of seasons.

It is pointless, however, to complain that the builders of Stonehenge would not have been able to possess the knowledge to construct such a sophisticated instrument of astronomical observation. The existence of Stonehenge itself is testimony to the skills of these "primitive" people. Prehistoric people were not subhuman brutes; they were men and women like you and me with the same intellectual capacities. Living in the stone or bronze age, with the knowledge available then, I certainly could not have planned the construction of Stonehenge, but living in modern times I could not develop the Theory of Relativity either. Who is to say that the genius of some prehistoric Einstein did not lay behind Stonehenge?

Recently a British archaeological writer named Patrick Crampton has challenged the whole idea that Stonehenge was a temple constructed by farmers and merchant princes. In his book *Stonehenge of the Kings* Crampton argues that the description of Stonehenge as a temple is a relic of "Victorian days, with its obsession with the religion of the ancients . . ."

"I believe," writes Crampton, "that in an extraordinary subtle way the dead hand of Victorian romanticism had continued to lead our thoughts almost exclusively down the paths of religion, diverting attention from the everyday life of the people."

And what was everyday life like?

The Wessex People were not "merchant princes," they were sea-roving robbers like the heroes of Homer's epics.

Rather than worshiping at Stonehenge, these warrior people actually lived in it. It was the capital of a bronze age warrior kingdom. "I see the populations of the tribal capitals living in drum-tower timber forts, two or more storeys high, some of the henges and barrows being the surviving remains of these." Unfortunately, Crampton gives no details on how the stones of Stonehenge were supposed to fit in with this new concept. Moreover, at Stonehenge itself, there is not a trace of a timber structure. Evidence of such structures have been found at other prehistoric British sites, and Crampton's town-fort theory may work there, but unless a fuller explanation is forthcoming, it doesn't work at Stonehenge.

Stonehenge is unique, but it is by no means the only famous prehistoric monument in Britain. Not far from Stonehenge is the great earthwork and stone circle of Avebury. The bank and ditch were much higher than at Stonehenge and encompassed a much greater area, being nearly fifteen hundred feet in diameter. Inside the bank there once stood a circle of about a hundred sarsens. They were not finished like those at Stonehenge, but the builders seem to have been careful to choose natural stones of a particular shape. Two or perhaps three smaller circles of sarsens stood inside the main circle, and huge boulders were placed on either side of the avenue leading to one of the four entrances to the circle.

The earthwork now surrounds the village of Avebury, built in medieval times, and it is in such a ruinous condition that for many years people were unaware of the ancient structure. It was rediscovered by John Aubrey in 1646. However, earlier people must have known of it, and perhaps tried to destroy it. Archaeologists found the body of a fourteenth-century man crushed under one of the stones. A pair of scissors under the bones indicate that he was probably a barber. The theory is that the man was killed while trying to tip over the stone. The gods of Avebury had their revenge.

Avebury was built about the same time as Stonehenge II. Avebury is close to Marlborough Downs and the same kind of sarsen sandstone was used. The sarsens for Stonehenge could well have been dragged through Avebury on their way to Salisbury Plain. Druidophile William Stukeley believed he had found an ancient road between Stonehenge and Avebury, but no one else has been able to locate it.

In 1928 archaeologists found another henge-type monument two miles from Stonehenge. This discovery was a triumph of modern archaeology, for the monument contains no stones, and its circular earthwork had been so flattened by plowing that it can not be seen from the ground. It was located by studying aerial photographs. Inside the earthwork, excavators found six concentric rings of circular holes for wooden posts. The remains of some of these posts still survived underground. Since nothing remains above the surface, we can only guess what it looked like, but according to archaeologist Atkinson, "The most sensible explanation is that the posts formed the upright framework of a roofed building, like a huge barn bent around upon itself into a circle, leaving a space open to the sky in the centre."

Then there are the barrows generally thought to be grave mounds. The Stonehenge area is littered with them. Says Atkinson, ". . . this concentration, like the grouping of graves round a church, must reflect the great sanctity of the district from Neolithic times onwards." They are basically of two types—long barrows, large communal graves, that probably were burial places for the Windmill Hill People, and round barrows, smaller burials for individuals. The custom of individual burial was probably introduced by the Beaker People.

About a half mile north of Stonehenge is a mysterious earthwork, the Curses. It is (or was, for most of it has been obliterated in modern times, but archaeologists are able to determine with a fair degree of accuracy what it looked like) a narrow enclosure almost two miles in length, bounded on either side by a low bank and ditch. It is much like Stonehenge's Avenue, but it doesn't seem to lead anywhere. Similar earthworks are found elsewhere in Britain, the longest being six miles. The Curses was probably built about the same time as Stonehenge I. No one knows what its purpose was. The best guess is that it was some sort of ceremonial way, for processions connected with rites at some of the barrows in the area.

Of all the monuments in Wiltshire the most enigmatic is

Silbury Hill. It is some sixteen miles north of Stonehenge, and has been called the Great Pyramid of Europe. It is conical in shape, 130 feet high, and its base covers five and one half acres. The mound is built entirely of chalk rubble. If it is not quite the Great Pyramid, it is surely the largest artificial mound in Europe. It does not have the technical sophistication of Stonehenge, but it probably took longer to build. Archaeologists estimate that some fifty million basketfuls of chalk, weighing thirty pounds each, had to be carried up the growing hill. Hawkins thinks it took three million man-days of labor. No one has been able to determine when it was built, but it was before the coming of the Romans, because a Roman road, which otherwise runs straight as an arrow, swerves to avoid its base. Most scholars assume it was completed about the time of Stonehenge.

What was the purpose of this massive mound? There is not a clue. In 1777 a shaft was dug from the top right through to the underlying chalk, but nothing of significance was found. Seventy-five years later another tunnel was dug from one side to join up with the shaft, again no results. Silbury Hill looks, more than anything else, like an enormous round barrow. But who could be buried there? Further excavations are planned.

Wiltshire is uniquely rich in stone and bronze age monuments, but it is not the only place in the world that possesses them. There are thousands of various types throughout Europe. Most of them have not been investigated very thoroughly, and many more doubtless remain unrecognized.

On the remote Isle of Lewis, northernmost of the Outer Hebrides, is a stone circle called Callanish. Gerald Hawkins believes that this too possesses astronomical alignments similar to, although less advanced, than those of Stonehenge.

Strangely, the remote northern islands, which today can support only tiny populations, seem to be exceptionally well endowed with stone age monuments, indicating that their population in prehistoric times was greater than it is today.

In the little town of Carnac, on the southern coast of Brittany, local legend speaks of an army of petrified Roman soldiers. Nearby there are three stone armies, columns of stones called menhirs (stone men) which range from two to twelve feet in height. They are arranged in perfect rows, and the largest of these groupings still contains over a thousand stones. In each case the monuments are connected with burials, which must have been of great importance, and in each case the rows of stones line up with the sunrise on midsummer's day.

Obviously the stereotype of prehistoric man, as a naked shambling savage living out his short life in tribal isolation, is in need of drastic revision. Conquerors and merchants ranged far, and now the archaeologists have been able to find the first faint traces of what might have been a great prehistoric missionary movement. The hints have been found in the massive stone tombs which in England are called long barrows. Similar tombs, are found throughout Europe, from Cyprus to Sweden, and some believe that the same sort of tomb building spread eastward as far as China. This megalithic tomb building seems to have started in the Mediterranean region and then spread widely and rather quickly among peoples of very different cultures. The only thing these far-flung people seem to have had in common was the way they buried their dead. Geoffrey Bibby sums up the opinion of many archaeologists: "Clearly, some religion, of which the most permanent feature was the construction of massive stone tombs for communal burial, had been spread from the East by a comparatively small body of proselytizers, too small to make any appreciable mark on the material culture of the settlements to which they came but with an influence great enough to bring about the adoption by their hosts of the new spiritual ideas." He draws a parallel with the efforts of the Christian missionaries in Africa and Asia during the nineteenth century.

Prehistoric archaeology is a new field, and techniques are improving all the time. The archaeologists have even wisely left parts of Stonehenge unexcavated, in the confident expectation that future diggers will have more sophisticated techniques at their command, and thus be able to make more of the opportunity.

There can be little doubt that even Stonehenge, the most thoroughly studied of all prehistoric monuments, still holds surprises. Although Stonehenge has been seen by millions, it was not until 1953 that one of the most startling discoveries about it was made, and then it was quite by accident. In June near sunset one of the excavators noticed that the oblique rays of the sun outlined some peculiar carvings on one of the great sarsens. The carvings were so shallow, that only under those specific lighting conditions could they be seen at all, and that is how they had escaped detection. They are easily visible today, having been worn more deeply in the stone by the fingers of visitors, intent on tracing their outline. They were carvings of axes and a dagger.

The ax carvings were similar to those found upon megalithic structures throughout northern Europe. But the dagger was of a very particular type, a type unknown in northern Europe. This sort of dagger was common in Greece around 1500 B.C. The Greeks of the time had an advanced bronze age culture. We call them Mycenaean Greeks, but they could also be called Homeric, for these are the people of Homer's epics.

The Mycenaean Greeks were more advanced than the people who built Stonehenge, and were experts at building massive stone structures. The similarities in the stone-working at Stonehenge and Mycenae have often been noted. All this raises an interesting bit of speculation. Was it possible that the Wessex People imported a Mycenaean architect to supervise the building of their great temple? We do know they had many contacts with the centers of higher civilization. Beads from Egypt have been found in their tombs. We also know the Greeks have always been great travelers, but what could induce a skilled artisan from Greece to come to the far North to supervise a public works project among the barbarians? Atkinson poses this answer: "A barbarian British king, whose voice and gifts spoke loudly enough to be heard even in the cities of the Mediterranean."

It is not unreasonable to assume that the final construction of Stonehenge took place when southern Britain was under the control of an extremely powerful overlord. It is the only important monument ever assigned to the Wessex People. For the most part they seem to have lived in a society made of rival clans, who could not get together long enough for a great communal venture, as Stonehenge obviously was. Stonehenge III must have been constructed during an unusual period of peace. "And how," asks Atkinson, "in such a society is peace imposed except from above?"

Atkinson believes that Stonehenge is evidence of concentration of power in the hands of a single man. "Who he was, whether he was native-born or foreign, we shall never know . . . Yet who but he should sleep . . . in the quiet darkness of a sarsen vault beneath the mountainous pile of Silbury Hill?"

Why did the excavations fail to reveal this vault? We must

recall that the builders of the pyramids of Egypt concealed the chambers in which the bodies of their great kings were placed. Would the Wessex People have done less for the body of their great king?

FIVE

ARTHUR'S BRITAN

Island of the Sleeping King

The British Isles are dotted with places associated with the name of King Arthur. From Land's End in the southwestern-most part of England to the Grampian Hills in the Highlands of Scotland, one can find an astonishing variety of places named after Arthur: Arthur's Seat, Arthur's Table, Arthur's Oven, Arthur's Island, and so forth. Two of the most cele-brated places are located almost at opposite ends of the map of Britain. Halfway down the rocky coast of Cornwall stands the impressive ruins of Tintagel Castle, reputed to be the birth-place of King Arthur. In Edinburgh a stark cliff called Arthur's Seat overlooks the Palace of Holyrood, the royal residence in Scotland.

Most of these places have nothing whatever to do with Arthur. But there are three important places connected with the legends of this British king that bear closer examination. The first, and by far the most famous today, is Camelot, Arthur's capital.

In recent years, primarily because of a musical comedy of that name, the search for Camelot has become almost synonymous with the search for King Arthur. But Camelot does not really figure too importantly in the Arthurian legends. During the middle ages, everybody was looking for Arthur's grave, or at least the place where Arthur slept until being called upon to again lead the Celts of Britain. This spot was the Isle of Avalon. Historians, however, have been most interested in locating a place called Badon Hill where Arthur fought his most important battle.

Are these places worth looking for at all? Was there a real King Arthur?

The American myth-collector Thomas Bullfinch says, "Arthur was a prince of the tribe of Britons called Silures . . . the son of Uther, named Pendragon, a title given to an elective sovereign, paramount over the many kings of Britain. He appears to have commenced his martial career about the year 500, and was raised to the Pendragonship about ten years later. He is said to have gained twelve victories over the Saxons . . ." The identification is by no means that certain.

Arthur's origins are lost in the darkest part of the dark ages in Britain. The last contacts with the Roman Empire had been unwillingly severed in the 450s. An aristocracy of native Britons, who had adopted the names and manners of Romans, was trying to hold on to a Roman way of life. It was one of those periods in history when enormous masses of people suddenly seem to be on the move. Rome itself was falling to pieces under the repeated attacks from restless barbarian tribes, and Britain, once Rome's most distant province, was being pressed by a variety of barbarians—Picts and Irish from the north and the Saxons and their allies, the Angles, Jutes and Frisians, from the Continent.

Ultimately the Saxons conquered almost all of what is now England, and it is from the records of the victors that we get our picture of the period. The documents called the *Anglo-Saxon Chronicles* describe the invasion as an unbroken march from victory to victory. They do not mention Arthur, who should have been their chief enemy. But even from these one-sided records, one catches hints that the victory was not as sweeping or as easy as the invaders wished to make it sound. There are gaps, at points where the invasion, for some unspecified reason, seemed to falter.

Fortunately there is another source for records of this period. The barbarians were, for the most part, pagans (although they converted rapidly once they settled down), but the Britons had adopted the Christianity of Rome, and records from church sources give a fuller account of the native resistance.

The earliest church record that has any bearing on the time of Arthur is *The Destruction and Conquest of Britain*, attributed to a Breton monk called Gildas. It was written a century or less after the time of Arthur. It has been suggested that Gildas himself was alive at Arthur's time. The trouble is that although Gildas writes of some of the events and personalities that were later incorporated into the stories of Arthur, he never mentions Arthur. True, Gildas leaves much to be desired as a historian. He is more of a religious polemicist intent on flailing away at the British kings whom he regarded as immoral backsliders. Still, this bothersome omission is the greatest single stumbling block in the way of accepting the historical reality of Arthur.

The next significant surviving record is the *History of the Church of England*, written by an English monk known as the Venerable Bede in the eighth century. Bede was living in a country completely under the control of the former bar-barians and was probably descended from them himself. He too had a poor opinion of the Celtic Britons, but he does name many British kings. Unfortunately again, Arthur is not among them.

In fact, there is no record of Arthur until the ninth century, a full three hundred years after the time he was supposed to have lived. At that time Nennius, a cleric in the household of the Bishop of Bangor, set about compiling *Historia Brittonum*, *The History of the Britons*. He relies heavily on Gildas and Bede, but makes one memorable addition to their stories. After telling of the death of Ambrosius, a British king mentioned by both the earlier writers, he describes the career of the man who took over command of the army.

"Arthur fought against the Saxon alongside the kings of the Britons, but he himself was the leader in the battles. The first battle was at the mouth of the river which is called Glein . . . The twelfth was on Mount Badon, in which—on that one day—there fell in one onslaught of Arthur's, nine hundred and sixty men; and none slew them but he alone, and in all his battles he remained victor."

In an appendix to his work, which Nennius calls *Mirabila*— Marvels—he mentions two associated with Arthur. The first concerns a heap of stones "in the region which they call Buelt." The topmost stone contained an imprint of the foot of Arthur's dog Cabal. Arthur himself piled up the heap of stones "and called it Carn Cabal."

"And men will come and carry away that stone for a day and a night, and the next morning there it is back again on its heap."

At another spot there is the burial mound of Arthur's son. "Arthur himself killed him there and buried him. And when men come to measure the length of the mound, they find it sometimes six feet, sometimes nine, sometimes twelve and sometimes fifteen. Whatever length you find it at one time you will find it different at another, and I myself have proved this to be true."

Nennius is so full of miracles and wonders, it is hard to know how far to trust him. But he did not make these stories up himself. He admits he is no writer, and his patchwork narrative reads more like a scrapbook than the invention of a single man. Nennius is a collector of old facts and legends that passed as facts. He undoubtedly had access to documents and oral traditions that are lost today.

Nennius' account shows that three centuries after his death, Arthur was a great hero and had assumed many of the characteristics which were to be so elaborately embroidered by later tradition. He was a Christian warrior of superhuman strength, he possessed magical powers, but he was not yet a king. Nennius refers to Arthur as *dux bellorum,* a title which may roughly be translated as "commander-in-chief." It is probably an old Roman military rank which the British continued to use.

In addition to Nennius, there are two other important early references to Arthur. The first is in the tenth-century *Annales Cambriae,* which records two of Arthur's battles. The battle of Badon in 518, "in which Arthur carried the cross of Our Lord Jesus Christ, for three days and three nights on his shoulders, and the Britons were victors." And in 539, "The battle of Camlaun in which Arthur and Medraut were slain; and there was death in England and Ireland."

The final reference to Arthur before Geoffrey of Monmouth, the first great chronicler of Arthurian lore, appears in the work of the twelfth-century writer William of Malmesbury. William is no soft-headed romantic. He is a skeptical, sharp-eyed historian and one tends to trust his account.

William complains about ". . . that Arthur of whom the trifling of the Britons talk so much nonsense even today; a man clearly worthy not to be dreamed of in fallacious fables, but to be proclaimed in veracious histories, as one who long sustained his tottering country, and gave the shattered minds of his fellow citizens an edge for war. Finally, at the siege of Mount Badon, relying upon the image of the mother of the Lord which he had sewn upon his armour, he [charged] singlehanded against nine hundred of the enemy and routed them with incredible slaughter."

This is all that has survived in writing and from these scanty materials we must draw at least a tentative picture of the hero Arthur.

He was born near the end of the fifth century and was either of direct Roman descent or came from an aristocratic Celtic family that was closely identified with the Romans. A good deal of fuss has been made about his name. Those who think he is purely a mythical figure say the name is a corruption of Artur, a pre-Christian god. Others who wish to link Arthur more closely to Rome believe the name was really Artorius. Still others believe that Arthur is merely a confused reference to Ambrosius Aurelianus, the ruler of that time who is mentioned prominently by Gildas. None of this confusion about the name is really necessary. Arthur is not a common name in early Celtic records, but it does appear now and then.

Arthur was probably appointed war leader by Ambrosius, to whom he may have been related. He managed to rouse the sagging spirits of his badly defeated countrymen and win a series of impressive victories against the Saxons and their allies. One theory is that his success was due to his knowledge of the Roman arts of war, particularly the employment of armored horsemen. The popular picture of Arthur and his knights going into battle looking like a group of tanks, completely encased in armor, is false. This cumbersome method of warfare did not come into use until the middle ages. When medieval writers took up the Arthur stories, they merely dressed the hero in the fighting garb of their own time. At best Arthur would have worn an iron cap and mail shirt, and his horse might have been lightly armored. Still, the barbarians had nothing like this. A well-coordinated armored cavalry charge by a small group of horsemen could easily spread panic among the numerous, but poorly disciplined barbarian troops.

Arthur was killed in battle around 540, not by the Saxons but in a dispute with members of his own family.

We know that after the middle of the sixth century the Saxon conquest picked up tempo, until they controlled virtually all of what is now present-day England. They held their control until routed by the Normans, another group of invaders from the Continent, five centuries later. The native Celts were not exterminated. They fled in large numbers to the more inaccessible or undesirable regions of Wales or Scotland. (Present-day Welshmen and Scotsmen resent being called Anglo-Saxons.) The majority, however, were submerged beneath a Saxon ruling class, with whom they thoroughly intermingled over the centuries. Really old traditions about Arthur are strongest in Celtic Wales and Scotland. But he seems to have been an underground hero, even in the Saxon-dominated lands. The Saxons, and later the Normans, ultimately fell under the spell of this ancient warrior, once their battle was finally won and the old antagonisms had time to die down. Much the same sort of thing happened during the Victorian era, when the English public, and the Queen herself, paid homage to that romantic adventurer Bonnie Prince Charlie, although it had been the Prince's aim to depose the Queen's own ancestors. A dead hero whose cause is irrevocably lost never lacks for supporters.

The first to exploit the Arthur stories for their literary value was the twelfth-century writer Geoffrey of Monmouth in his *History of the Kings of Britain.* Geoffrey claimed to have used as his source an ancient book in the British language. Some scholars doubt if any such book ever existed. Geoffrey culled from many sources, English, Irish, Welsh, French, classical and Biblical, besides relying heavily on his own imagination.

It was Geoffrey who introduced Merlin, attributing to him the deeds of an earlier wonder-worker mentioned by Nennius. The source of the magician's strange name is unknown and has been the subject of an obscure but seemingly endless scholarly debate. One guess is that Merlin is a corruption of the name of a pagan god.

In the centuries that followed, Arthur was elevated from the position of *dux bellorum* of the Britons to a place alongside Alexander the Great and Charlemagne as one of the great heroes of medieval Europe. Simple stories were altered and elaborated upon with infinite variation. Whole cycles of supplementary legends were tacked on as the adventures of Arthur's knights. The amount of literature produced about King Arthur is staggering.

The story of Arthur was given its best and most complete rendering by Sir Thomas Malory in the fifteenth century. Malory was a country gentleman from Warwickshire, in central England. He is a character right out of the Arthur stories—one of the evil characters. His quick temper and fierce nature landed him in prison eight times. (He made two daring escapes, once reportedly swiming a moat in full armor.) When he was free he robbed and murdered with an abandon considered excessive even in that lawless era. But during periods of forced inactivity, while languishing in prison, he turned his thoughts to the deeds of Arthur, the king who had tried so hard to establish the rule of law in his domain. Malory composed what he described as "the whole book of King Arthur and his noble knights of the Round Table." The book is a combination of several French romances which Malory freely translated into English. It was published in 1485 and is generally known under the French title *Le Morte d'Arthur*.

In Malory's book, Arthur and his knights go clattering about in heavy armor, having all sorts of magical adventures, rescuing maidens in distress and obeying all the elaborate rules of medieval chivalry. After Malory, the cast of characters— Queen Guinevere, her lover Sir Lancelot, the wizard Merlin, the ambitious Mordred, and the unfailingly noble King Arthur—are fixed. Later, more delicate writers cleaned up Malory's tales a bit, for chivalry to Malory was not the pallid, sexless thing of the Victorians, but no major changes were made. The characters of the musical *Camelot* are far more Malory and the French romances than they are Arthur himself.

Despite all the problems connected with establishing the existence of Arthur in the first place, *Debrett's Peerage*, the *Who's Who* of British aristocracy, has recently linked Arthur with the reigning queen, Elizabeth II.

Debrett's editor, P. W. Montague-Smith, traces the line to Cunedda, a fifth-century Scottish king who started a royal dynasty in North Wales. His granddaughter, says Montague-Smith, was Elgir, Arthur's mother; and members of his family were the ancestors of the House of Tudor, from which the present Elizabeth is vaguely descended.

The task of locating the places associated with Arthur is infinitely more difficult than it first seemed, because he was not a great king of high middle ages, but more probably a war leader in a period of decline and darkness. Yet it is not an entirely impossible task.

We can start by looking for the place where Arthur was born. The first person to name a birthplace is the notoriously unreliable Geoffrey. This is Geoffrey's story: The king of England, Uther Pendragon (also brother of the King Ambrosius Aurelianus), tricked the wife of the Duke of Tintagel into sleeping with him with the aid of a bit of Merlin's magic. The child born from this union was Arthur.

There is a very real Tintagel Castle, and its picturesquely crumbling ruins can be found on the northern coast of Cornwall. The castle stands on a rocky cliff overlooking the sea; indeed, much of it has, over the years, fallen into the sea. What remains is wildly romantic. Such splendid ruins fire the imagination with scenes of Arthur and his knights riding out to battle. Local hotel owners and shopkeepers are keenly aware of the powerful attraction of their ruin with its Arthurian associations, and the casual tourist may leave Tintagel thinking he has seen the remains of the castle of Camelot itself. It isn't Camelot, of course, and no one ever seriously said it was. Tintagel can't even be Arthur's birthplace, because it was built a good seven centuries after he died. The present castle dates from the thirteenth century. It was constructed on the foundation of an older castle, but even this does not go back to Arthurian times. The oldest known building on the site is a monastery, hardly the place for Uther's amorous adventure. Tintagel is out.

Erick Chambers, a student of Arthurian lore, believes that "the vagrant fancy of Geoffrey of Monmouth had put Arthur at Tintagel." He finds no connection between Arthur and Tintagel, prior to Geoffrey. "And when an antiquarian came to Tintagel with Geoffrey's book in his pocket and asked for traces of the hero, one may be sure that the complaisance of the native guide would supply his need."

This is not to imply that Cornwall is entirely without solid Arthurian associations. Near the town of Fowey, there is a battered seven-foot stone pillar which contains an inscription in Latin: "Here lies Drustans, son of Cunomorus." Drustans is a form of the name Tristram, and Tristram is one of Arthur's most celebrated knights. Cunomorus may be an early Cornish king, Marcus Quonomorius, or the King Mark of the Arthur stories. In the stories, Tristram was Mark's nephew.

Any attempt to establish Arthur's true birthplace is probably hopeless. A more fruitful area for investigation are the sites of his battles, for they go back to Nennius. The problem here is that Nennius' place names are entirely meaningless to us, and if he got them from old British records as he claimed, they were probably meaningless to him too. Some believe that all the battles were fought in Scotland, others place them at scattered points around the map, by finding vague similarities between the names Nennius gives and those by which the different places have been known.

However, from what is known about the advance of the Saxons, most scholars place the important battle action of Arthurian times in southeast England in the counties of Wiltshire and Somerset. The Saxons had landed in the west and moved steadily eastward up the Thames valley. They may have encountered the Wansdyke, an enormous defensive line made up of a bank and ditch running fifty miles from the

Bristol Channel, through the Marlborough Downs, to a spot known as Inkpen. Many assume this great rampart was constructed under the direction of Ambrosius. In truth, we don't known who constructed it, or when, but it is in the right spot to have been a Celtic line of defense.

Most speculation has centered in the location of Mount Badon or Badon Hill, for it seems to be the site of Arthur's most important victory. In addition to Nennius, Gildas and Bede mention the battle of Badon Hill, although they do not attribute the victory to Arthur. The Britons probably launched their successful counterattack from a hill fort, which gave its name to the battle.

There are several likely locations. The most promising is an ancient fortification called Liddington Castle, just outside of the town of Swindon, which is some seventy miles west of London. A Saxon army, moving up the lower Thames toward Wiltshire and Somerset and taking the easiest line of advance, would have to pass right by Liddington Castle. A defeat at that point would have been highly significant.

Proponents of this identification have solved the name problem by finding a place which once bore the name of Badbury close by. Their thinking runs thus: If Badbury could have been changed to Badon, then Liddington could have been confused with its neighbor Badbury.

The fortifications at Liddington are hardly deserving of the name "castle." They are a series of earthen ramparts on the western shoulder of Liddington Hill, a ridge rising nine hundred feet above sea level. There are many earthworks in the area, indicating that many battles had been fought there in many ages, but those on Liddington Hill are the most formidable.

This is the battle of Badon Hill as it might have been: The

Saxons knew that Arthur and his men were encamped in the fortifications atop the hill and that from that position they were immune to attack. But attack was unnecessary. The Saxons had a much larger force and could simply bypass Badon and strike at more poorly defended targets farther on. They prepared to march on past but had to go by way of a narrow gap in the ridge under the hill. As the barbarians crowded hastily into the gap, Arthur and his mounted cavalry suddenly charged down the gentler slopes of the hill into the midst of the Saxons, who by now were pushing every which way to avoid the charge of the armored men. It was terrifying. The Saxons were seasoned warriors, but they had never experienced the lightning blow of a well-disciplined cavalry charge. Arthur himself was in the lead, carrying on his shoulders the cross of his God. The Saxons must have known and respected, even feared, this Briton soldier because of his other victories. The cross, too, must have inspired fear. The pagans could hardly have been unaware of the stories of the powers of this talisman. As individual fighters, no man in the world could be considered superior in bravery or ferocity to a Saxon. But they were a collection of individual warriors, not a disciplined army. The great weakness of all barbarian forces is that once panic begins they have no training and no authority to hold them back.

Arthur and his men charged, regrouped and charged the fleeing barbarians again and again. The Saxon confusion was so great that the Celtic horsemen rode among them killing at will. When the battle was over, the Saxons had left the majority of their force dead on the field. Many had been killed by Arthur's men, many more had been crushed and trampled in their attempt to squeeze out of the narrow gap in the ridge that had so suddenly become a death trap.

Camelot, Arthur's main headquarters, was inserted into the legend cycle by French romancers. Malory included it in his account, and it has grown in importance since that time. The French may have made the name up or obtained it from older documents, but it is impossible to locate Camelot on the basis of its name alone. Malory himself put Camelot at Winchester. This is hardly a serious identification. There was a famous castle at Winchester in Malory's time—some of it is still there—but it is too new. Winchester Castle was built by William the Conqueror long after Arthurian times. Besides, Winchester is much too far south and west.

However, if you want to see the Round Table, or at least a round table, you can find the top of a very nice one hanging in the great hall of the castle at Winchester. The whole idea of Arthur's Round Table is a late invention, apparently inserted in the stories by a Norman poet named Wace.

The table at Winchester is a fine relic. It is made of worn oak planks and is eighteen feet in diameter. At the top of the table there is a picture of a medieval Arthur, seated upon his throne, scepter in hand. The rest of the table is painted in a spoke pattern in twenty-four alternating bands of white and green. At the end of each spoke are the names of Arthur's most celebrated knights. It is too perfect not to be a fake.

The table top itself may go back as far as the twelfth century, but the painting was commissioned by Henry VIII, in the sixteenth century. Henry was extremely anxious to identify his line with the great hero. (The Arthur legend was very strong at the time and Henry's older brother, who died before attaining the throne, was named Arthur. England narrowly missed having a real, identifiable King Arthur.) Henry had the table painted green and white, his family colors.

During the fourteenth century, Edward III of England

and Philip VI of France both tried to build round tables, but they abandoned their projects as impractical. Henry VIII had been willing to settle for a mere twenty-four at table. But according to the stories Arthur had at least 150 knights. To have seated all of them comfortably, the Round Table would have had to have been at least 125 feet in diameter. Such a monstrosity could never have been fitted into a fourteenth-century castle. A special hall would have been needed to contain it.

The real origins of the name Camelot are lost. A philological guess is that it came from Camulodunum (modern Colchester), capital of a heroic pre-Roman British king, Cunobelin. Perhaps it did, but Camulodunum is in the extreme southeast, and there is a much more promising location for Camelot right where it should be, in the southwest, in Somerset.

Right now the search for Camelot is centered at a place called variously Cadbury Hill, Cadbury Camp or Cadbury Castle. Three miles away are the villages of Queen's Camel and West Camel, named from the stream once called Cam. Many Celtic streams were named Cam, which means "the crooked."

Cadbury Hill contains another of those ancient earthworks that once served as fortresses. Archaeologists digging at the site have found that the earliest traces of human habitation date back four thousand years, to the stone age. The archaeologists also found traces of a line of trenches which puzzled them greatly until they discovered that the hill had been used by the British Army for maneuvers during the First World War.

In between these two extremes in time the hill had been used by the early Britons and their Roman conquerors. The most significant new discovery is that the walls of the fortress were heavily refortified early in the sixth century—Arthur's time. During that period, Cadbury Hill must have contained the most formidable military installation in southwest England.

The archaeologists didn't have to tell the local people that they were living near Camelot; their grandfathers told them that. The ghost of King Arthur was everywhere. Fifty years ago locals could show you King Arthur's Well, in the lowest rampart of the earthwork, and his palace, a natural elevation at the crest. Then, you could still hear the story of the silver shoe from Arthur's horse that was dug up in the palace, told by people who believed it.

"Folks do say that on the night of the full moon King Arthur and his men ride round the hill, and their horses are shod with silver, and a silver shoe has been found in the track where they do ride, and when they have ridden round the hill, they stop to water their horses at the Wishing Well."

In another story Arthur and his men come riding down from the hill on Christmas Eve to drink from a well by the village church.

The hill itself was reputed to be hollow and could be entered by iron or golden gates. In the 1890s there was a local who claimed to have seen these gates as a child but he could not quite recall where they were. If you looked through the gates on St. John's Eve, according to a traditional poem, you could see the king sitting in the middle of his court. But there was something malevolent about the tradition and no one had the courage to put it to the test. When a group of antiquaries visited the hill around the turn of the century, one old man asked them if they had come to take the king away.

An interesting recent archaeological find at Cadbury Hill was fragments of pottery wine jars that must have been imported all the way from the eastern Mediterranean. This indicates that during the early sixth century Cadbury Hill was the home of a very important and powerful chieftain. But was he Arthur, and was Cadbury Camelot? The theory has gained a lot of supporters in England, and work at the site is continuing. But barring some really extraordinary find, the question will probably remain open. Past excavations of early Celtic sites have found them disappointingly bare of personal objects. So no one is really expecting to uncover Arthur's sword or helmet. Cadbury Hill could have been Camelot, but we simply do not know.

The Cam and Camels near Cadbury conjure up another Arthurian association. This place has often been identified as Camlan (or Camlaun), the site of Arthur's final fatal battle with his kinsman Medraut or Mordred. Almost all we have to go on is the similarity in names and Camlan might just as well be named from the Camel River near Camelford; indeed, Geoffrey of Monmouth chose the Camel, although he does not give his reasons. Cadbury, however, has a group of graves huddled at its foot which may indicate an ancient battle.

What makes the Cadbury-Camlan identification so intriguing is that Cadbury is quite near the ruins of Glastonbury Abbey, long thought to be the burial place of Arthur. An ancient pathway runs between the two spots, and legend has it that people "sometimes, on rough winter nights, heard King Arthur and his hound go by along that track."

A visitor to the ruins of Glastonbury will find this sign on the grounds: "SITE OF KING ARTHUR'S TOMB. In the year 1191 the bodies of King Arthur and his Queen were said to have been found on the south side of the Lady Chapel. On the 19th of April 1278 their remains were removed in the presence of King Edward and Queen Eleanor to a black marble tomb on this site. This tomb survived until the dissolution of the Abbey in 1539."

The site of what may have been Arthur's original grave has been identified in the old Celtic cemetery on the Abbey grounds, but it has yielded nothing of importance, and the identification may well be false. The black marble tomb of the reburial and its contents have been entirely destroyed, so archaeology can be of little use in confirming the truth of the tradition that Arthur was buried at Glastonbury. But the tradition is strong, compelling, and dramatically satisfying.

The early references to Arthur's last resting place are extremely mysterious. An ancient but undated document called the *Song of Graves* contains an obscure line which has been translated "A mystery to the world, the grave of Arthur." Geoffrey of Monmouth tells of Arthur's last battle but says that he was not killed, only badly wounded, and that his surviving knights carried him away to the Island of Avalon, where his wounds were to be healed. A dominant feature of Welsh mythology is that Arthur is not dead but merely sleeping, on the miraculous Isle of Avalon. Someday, the traditions say, Arthur will awaken, and like a Celtic messiah lead his people in the reconquest of their homeland. The idea that a great leader of the past is not dead, and will someday return, is common among defeated people. Geoffrey relied heavily on Welsh sources. Unfortunately he does not specify the location of the Island of Avalon, but his description does not sound like Glastonbury in Somerset.

Arthur's grave was first firmly placed at Glastonbury by Giraldus Cambrensis, who wrote at the end of the twelfth century. Giraldus was no great lover of Arthurian lore and was one of the first to ridicule Geoffrey's account. Giraldus says that while King Henry II was on a tour through Wales he learned from a wandering bard that Arthur was buried at a particular spot in Glastonbury, and that Glastonbury itself is the Isle of Avalon. The king passed this information on to the Abbot of Glastonbury, but the monks did nothing about it for a while. Then in 1191 there was a disastrous fire which destroyed most of the abbey. Shortly after that the monks excavated the site of the Celtic grave, and the bones of King Arthur and his queen were found and later reburied in a marble tomb, under the eyes of the reigning king. It sounds reasonable enough at first, but there is something disquietingly convenient about the way things were supposed to have happened. The monks themselves had to raise money for the rebuilding of the abbey after the fire, and finding the hero's grave resulted in a great deal of favorable publicity for Glastonbury. English kings, too, profited from the find, because they could claim to hold the throne once possessed by a universal hero, and at the same time put an end to the troublesome Welsh prophecies of Arthur's return and the reconquest of England by the Celts. If they had Arthur's bones, then he surely was not just sleeping. For these reasons, many have believed that Arthur's grave was merely a monkish forgery concocted with royal approval. But the question simply has to remain open since the evidence has been thoroughly destroyed.

Oddly, though, when the monks of Glastonbury made their astonishing announcement, the Welsh did not dispute it. Perhaps Welsh tradition held that Glastonbury was Arthur's burial place, as Giraldus' story of the Welsh bard seems to indicate.

A modern visitor might well wonder how Glastonbury could ever have been called the Isle of Avalon, or the isle of anything else, for it is clearly not an island. But Glastonbury consists of a series of small hills that once were surrounded by marshy lowlands—now drained—and were connected with dry land only by a narrow ridge. Thus it could be considered a proper inland island.

The area has been inhabited for a very long time. There is a theory (but no archaeological proof) that Glastonbury was used as a pagan sanctuary by the pre-Roman Celts at least as early as the third century B.C.

Glastonbury's associations with Christianity begin with the beginning of Christianity itself. Medieval traditions make the founder of the Old Church at Glastonbury, St. Joseph of Arimathea, the rich Jew who took Jesus' body and placed it in his own tomb. Early Christian sources have Joseph traveling off to found a church in some distant but unspecified land to the west. Later traditions make this place Glastonbury in Britain. It is stimulating to speculate on this possibility. Joseph was a rich man and a Roman subject. Britain was the most distant part of the Roman Empire. If Joseph wished to proselytize for his new religion in a place where he might be relatively free from persecution, he would have had the funds to travel to Britain. Such speculation proves nothing, of course; medieval writers might have thought along similar lines and set these thoughts down as facts.

St. Joseph of Arimathea gets mixed into the Arthurian legends because he was supposed to have carried with him the Holy Grail, which Arthur's knights spent so much time questing after. This is another connection between Arthur and Glastonbury, but an admittedly far-fetched one.

Our old friend William of Malmesbury is the principal historian of Glastonbury. He says nothing of St. Joseph of Arimathea. His account begins with King Lucius, a legendary British ruler of the second century, who was supposed to have visited Rome and to have returned with missionaries who converted the people and established the Old Church of St. Mary at Glastonbury. Although William seems ignorant of the connection with Joseph of Arimathea, he is aware of another tradition that the Old Church was founded by the disciples of Christ. William, who had little regard for the factual basis of this story, said he would "leave disputable matters and gird himself for the narration of solid fact." William does not put Arthur at Glastonbury, but alludes to a secret grave and to the prophesied return.

Archaeology cannot make fine enough distinctions to allow us to know when the first Christian house of worship was built at Glastonbury. All we can say is that it was among the earliest in Britain. Since Glastonbury may have been an important pagan center, it seems natural for Christian missionaries to usurp this spot, in order to root out the pagan beliefs. The many legends, which have holy hermits and saints driving devils and their supernatural companions from the heights of Glastonbury Tor, may reflect a struggle between the new religion and the old.

The concept of the Isle of Avalon is not a Christian one. It belongs to Celtic mythology. It is a burial place, an island of the dead, a Celtic Valhalla for dead heroes—the traditions are confused. There were probably many islands of the dead, of which an old pagan sanctuary at Glastonbury may have been one. This tradition could have survived the foundation of a Christian church, and ultimately merged with it.

Here then is how the mystery of Arthur's grave, and the Isle of Avalon, might have grown. Arthur is mortally wounded at Camlan and as a faithful Christian warrior he wishes to be buried at a holy place. The foremost and perhaps only Christian foundation in the vicinity is at Glastonbury. But Glastonbury is older than Christianity; there are folk memories of the island of the dead, the Isle of Avalon.

Very probably early Celtic Christianity did not run that deeply among the common people. To them it would have seemed right for the hero to be buried at a place sacred to the old gods as well as the new God.

Geoffrey Ashe, a British writer, in his book *Glastonbury, Arthur's Isle of Avalon* contends that the secrecy about Arthur's grave was deliberate.

"In view of the circumstances of Arthur's end—strife among his own people, while the Saxons were building up for a fresh advance—it may be that his lieutenants concealed their loss. Immediate publication would have dealt too heavy a blow to native morale, would have given too much encouragement to the enemy. A few loyal veterans . . . carried off the leader's body to some remote spot and buried it under cover of darkness, hoping that the heathen might be restrained a little longer by the power of his name and fear of his return . . ."

Ashe even makes a stab at explaining the greatest enigma of the Arthur legend, the silence of Gildas, the one chronicler who may have been alive at the time of Arthur. Others have said that Gildas did not know of Arthur because Arthur did not exist, or that Gildas was more interested in ecclesiastical matters than political events and simply overlooked Arthur, or that Arthur was connected with some heretical branch of Christianity, and the orthodox Gildas would not name such a man. But Ashe has another idea, "a final fancy," he calls it.

"Was Gildas present at the graveside? and did he swear secrecy with the rest? and did he avoid mentioning Arthur in his book because he had found that Arthurian reminiscences led to awkward questions?"

So there you have it. You can chase Arthur back and forth

across the map of the British Isles; everywhere he remains elusive. The legends are so numerous, and the evidence so scanty, that one is often tempted to conclude that there was no such person at all. Yet just because later poets and romancers clothed the hero in attributes that no mortal man could ever possess, there is no justification for using the foolish ornamentation as evidence against him. The unadorned stories about Arthur are not implausible, and the lack of material evidence is not surprising.

Just in case you think Arthur could not have existed because no one so universally believed to be good, fine, noble, honest and all the rest could ever have been a human being, it might help you to know that Arthur has not always been treated with respect. The legends have the evil Mordred joining up with the Picts against Arthur, and in the districts of ancient Pictland the stories make Mordred a hero and deprecate Arthur. Geoffrey and the others let Queen Guinevere off very lightly, in view of her sexual adventures. But the common people are much stricter in such matters. In parts of Wales at one time, you could get your face slapped for calling a girl a Guinevere. There is a rhyme:

> Guinevere Giant Ogurvan's daughter,
> Naughty young, more naughty later.

And from another Celtic district comes this rhyme:

> When King Arthur ruled this land,
>   He ruled it like a swine;
> He bought three pecks of barley meal
>   To make a pudding fine.
> His pudding it was nodden well,
>   And stuffed right full of plums;
> And lumps of suet he put in
>   As big as my two thumbs.

SIX

MOHENJO-DARO

Hill of the Dead

The three great early civilizations grew up in river valleys. Two are well known: the Egyptian in the valley of the Nile and the Sumerian in the valley of the Tigres and Euphrates. The third, which we may call Harappan, in the valley of the Indus River, is little known beyond archaeological circles. Even to the professionals the civilization of the Indus presents some of the greatest unsolved puzzles of the past.

For centuries this civilization was lost entirely. There were legends which described, quite forcefully, the fall of the great cities of the Indus, but until 1921 no one believed them. The nomadic Aryans conquered India about 1500 B.C. (The much abused term Aryan is what the conquering nomads called themselves. They spoke a language belonging to a family we call Indo-European, and Aryan is sometimes used loosely to describe all peoples who speak Indo-European languages. It seems hardly necessary to repeat once again that there is no such thing as an Aryan race.)

The descendants of the conquerors collected the hymns and poems of the days of the conquest and wrote them down in Sanscrit, an ancient Indo-European language. These writings are known collectively as the *Rig-Veda*, a term meaning sacred hymns of praise. They are among the oldest surviving religious writings, and are still held sacred by millions of Hindus.

The *Rig-Veda* contains some thousand hymns in praise of the numerous Hindu gods. One to Indra, the powerful war god (whose name is the basis for the word India), declares:

With all-outstripping chariot-wheel, O Indra, thou far famed, has
    overthrown the twice ten kings of men
With sixty thousand nine and ninety followers
Thou goest on from fight to fight intrepidly, destroying fort after
    fort here with strength.

Indra become "puramdara," "fort destroyer." He shatters "ninety forts." In another hymn, he demolishes ninety-nine "ancient castles" belonging to the enemy Sambora. He "rends forts as age consumes a garment." Forts "with a hundred walls" are mentioned.

Who built these forts? Where were the ruins? The *Rig-Veda* calls the pre-Aryan inhabitants of India "dasyas." They are described as a strange dark people. But of the locations of the forts and castles Indra and his followers overthrew, the *Rig-Veda* gives not a clue. Surely, the archaeologists reasoned, such a substantial civilization as described in the *Rig-Veda* could not have disappeared entirely—unless of course it never really existed. It was the general impression among scholars that the *Rig-Veda* was describing battles that never took place. The early Aryans had exaggerated the strength and accomplishments of their opponents in order to make their own victory appear greater.

A moderate and careful tone was adopted by John Marshall, Director General of Archaeology of India in the 1920s. In the *Cambridge History of India* he wrote:

"It is the misfortune of Indian history that its earliest and most obscure pages are able to derive little light from contemporary antiquities." Two years later he was announcing that members of his staff had discovered a prehistoric Indian civilization comparable to that of Sumer. These discoveries, said Marshall, were as important as the discoveries made by Heinrich Schliemann at Troy. And, says archaeologist Glyn Daniel "he was quite right."

This great discovery was not exactly new for the archaeologists realized—to their everlasting horror—that when they rode the railroad between Karachi and Lahore they were riding on rails set, in part, on crushed bricks made by the great pre-Aryan civilization mentioned in the *Rig-Veda.*

It was a practice of railroad builders in India to use city ruins as quarries for brick and stone with which to build up the rail bed. When the Karachi to Lahore run was being built in 1856, one of the project supervisors, William Brunton, found some old ruins near the modern village of Harappa. The ruins seemed worthless to the railroad man. They were located conveniently near the line, and one didn't have to dig very far to get to the necessary brick. A hundred miles of rail were laid on foundations of bricks that had been fired four thousand years ago. The railroad men had no idea of the age of the material they were digging out of the mound near Harappa. And it is doubtful that, even if they had known, it would have made much difference at the time.

Aside from bricks, they found little stone seals, some beautifully engraved with designs of real and mythical animals and other strange ornamentation. But very few showed an interest in the seals. There was no move to start archaeological excavations at Harappa. So the ruins were again abandoned to obscurity. The unwelcome attention of the railroad men had done more damage to them in a year than four thousand years of time and neglect.

Seventy years later, an Indian archaeologist on John Marshall's staff decided the mounds at Harappa were worth another look. As he dug, more seal stones and thousands upon thousands of bricks came to light. Here without doubt was a very large city, far older than any that had ever been dug up in India before, and completely unlike any other.

What the builders of the city called themselves is unknown. In such cases it is customary to name a culture after the place where traces of it were first recognized. Hence, the name Harappan. Interestingly, the *Rig-Veda* mentions a city called Hari-Yupuya. Could this ancient place name, only slightly altered, have been passed on through the centuries to a modern village? At present the question is unanswerable.

The following year, archaeologists began digging at a desolate group of mounds called Mohenjo-daro (the hill of the dead). These were located on the Indus River about four hundred miles downstream from Harappa. (The Indus flows through what is now Pakistan, and has been renamed the Sinder.) Harappa is actually on a tributary of the Indus, the Ravi. The finds at Mohenjo-daro were to be even more spectacular than those at Harappa, for although the two cities are virtually twins, Mohenjo-daro is in a much better state of preservation, having escaped the railroad builders. In addition, many smaller sites have been unearthed since the initial discoveries in 1921 and 1922.

How, one wonders, does a civilization as large as that of the Indus valley get lost, even in four thousand years, so that only the preserved boasts of its destroyers hint that it ever existed.

But upon viewing the remains of the Harappan cities, particularly Mohenjo-daro, an even more pressing question arises. How did civilization of any kind ever develop in such an awful place? Mohenjo-daro is located in a plain called the Sind. Parts of the Sind are rich grain-producing areas, and have been since ancient times. But throughout the Sind are patches of jungle and barren salt-covered desert.

Mohenjo-daro is located in one of these salt deserts. John Marshall, who excavated extensively at the site and grew to hate the region, paints a depressing picture:

"The salts which also permeate the soil of Sind have hastened the decay of the site. With the slightest moisture in the air, these salts crystallize on any exposed surface of the ancient brickwork, causing it to disintegrate and flake away, and eventually reducing it to powder. So rapid is their action that within a few hours after a single shower of rain newly excavated buildings take on a mantle of white rime like freshly fallen snow. The desolation that thus distinguishes this group of mounds is shared by the plain immediately around them, which for the most part is also white with salt and sustains little besides the dwarf tamarisk and the babul, the camel-thorn, and tussocks of coarse kanh grass. Add to this that the climate of the locality is one of the worst in India; that the temperature ranges from below freezing point to 120 degrees Fahrenheit; that there are bitterly cold winds in winter, frequent dust storms in summer; that the average rainfall is not more than 6 inches, but occasionally varied by torrential downpours; that clouds of sandflies and mosquitoes increase the discomforts of life—and it will be found hard to picture a less attractive spot than Mohenjo-daro is today."

Another archaeologist, Stuart Piggott, describes the salt as "a brittle shining crust that crushes beneath the step like a satanic mockery of snow. The whole landscape is whitened, and forms a dead background to the ugly stunted trees and grey-green bushes that stud the plain."

Historians have always believed that man needs a challenging environment before he can make the step from unorganized barbarism to organized civilized life. Neither the valley of the Nile, nor the valley of the Tigres and Euphrates, where the two other great ancient riverine civilizations developed, are entirely pleasant places. But the climate of the Mohenjo-daro area is far worse.

Archaeologists have decided that when Harappan civilization flourished the climate around Mohenjo-daro must have been better than it is now. Certainly there must have been more rain. The exterior walls of the city's buildings are made of kiln-dried or burnt brick. Today the people of the Sind and of all other dry areas in the Orient use mud brick, a much simpler, cheaper product that is dried in the sun. Mud brick is as good as burnt brick except for one feature. When there is a heavy rainfall, mud brick tends to melt and turn back into mud, while burnt brick survives. Had the climate in the days of Mohenjo-daro's greatness been as dry as it is today, the Harappans would scarcely have bothered with the trouble and expense of burnt brick.

Then, too, archaeologists have traced in the ruins elaborate drainage systems. A needless luxury today, but in a wetter era four thousand years ago perhaps a necessity.

What caused the change in climate? There are many theories. The Harappans themselves, by cutting down all their trees to feed the fires which baked their bricks, and by overcultivating the land, may have turned a once fertile, well-watered area into a salt-parched desert. Perhaps there was a change in the prevailing wind patterns or in the overall move-ment of air masses. There is some evidence that the flow of the Indus itself has changed—and that the land has risen over the centuries.

Mohanjo-daro and Harappa are some four hundred miles apart, but as far as archaeologists are able to determine, the two were built at the same time, under the same rigid plan. In addition, up to one hundred smaller settlements scattered over a thousand miles of the Indus valley have been linked to Harappan civilization. Despite all that has been discovered since 1921—and archaeological work in the Indus valley has been extensive—there remains something freakishly anony-mous and a bit chilling about Harappan civilization. A closer look at Mohenjo-daro, the best preserved of the Harrappan sites, quickly indicates why.

The mounds covering the ancient city we call Mohenjo-daro are quite visible from the flat river valley, the largest rising seventy feet from the floor of the plain. The ruins cover some 240 acres, but it is clear to excavators that the city was much larger. It has suffered greatly from centuries of floods and erosion.

What remains of Mohenjo-daro is not pleasant to behold. Writes John Marshall: "Anyone walking for the first time through Mohenjo-daro might fancy himself surrounded by the ruins of some present-day working town of Lancashire. This is the impression produced by the wide expanse of bare red brick structures, devoid of any semblance of ornament, and bearing in every feature the mark of stark utilitarianism ... The workaday appearance of the buildings and signal absence

of decoration is the more remarkable, because Indian archi-
tecture is notorious for the rich exhuberance of its ornament
and art of brick carving itself . . ."

The plan of Mohenjo-daro was laid out in advance. It is
perhaps the earliest example of city planning, and displays
some of its best and worst features. The residential section is
crossed by broad north-south streets. Somewhat smaller
streets cross at right angles to the main avenues, cutting the
area into large blocks. These blocks are subdivided by lanes
parallel or at right angles to the arterial streets. The houses
themselves are all constructed of excellent burnt brick, and
all follow the same pattern. They had two stories of tiny
rooms built around a courtyard. What windows there were
looked out onto the court, and the doors themselves opened
onto lanes rather than the main streets. Thus the streets of
Mohenjo-daro were bounded by block after block of blank
featureless brick wall. There may have been some sort of
ornamentation—wood carving perhaps—which has since perished, but this is just guessing.

Despite the dullness, there were advantages to living in
Mohenjo-daro. An elaborate system of drains indicate abundant water both for washing and sanitary purposes. Indeed,
the sanitary arrangements at Mohenjo-daro and the other
Harappan cities four thousand years ago seem better than
those in many places in the world today. In the ancient world
only the Minoan cities of Crete had "plumbing" equal to that
of the Harappan cities.

The layout of Mohenjo-daro was dominated by what we
call the Citadel. It was a thickly walled artificial mound, perhaps fifty feet high. The largest building on the Citadel was a
well-constructed granary. There is also an enormous tank or
bath, surrounded by a structure with many rooms, each of

which seemed to contain its own private bath. There is a building which excavators guess may have served as the residence of a priest or a college of priests.

Writes Mortimer Wheeler, a pioneer of the archaeology of India: ". . . the Citadel was both a religious and a secular headquarters; with the prototype of the ritual tanks of medieval and modern India, halls of assembly, and the State Granary which, in the economics of those times, may be equated with a modern State Bank."

Mohenjo-daro has now been almost entirely excavated. Not all the structures there have been identified, and there is some disagreement about details. One excavator sees conical hollows in a floor as dyeing vats, another believes them to be holders for large jars in a public restaurant. In one building with closely packed rooms, an excavator sees a college of priests; another viewing the same ruins sees them as the remains of a police station. But everyone agrees that several structures are missing. For example, no palace has been found. It may be one of the badly damaged and thus unidentifiable buildings on the Citadel, but this does not seem likely.

Another odd omission is a temple. The temple might be there, for on the Citadel of Mohenjo-daro stands a new Buddhist monastery—new, that is, in terms of the city's antiquity. The Buddhists started their building a mere seventeen hundred years ago. It is common for holy places of one culture to be built atop those of an earlier culture, so the Buddhists may have chosen the sacred ground of a vanished Harappan temple for their monastery. Mohenjo-daro was uninhabited for fifteen centuries before the Buddhists moved in, yet the memory of the holy spot may have persisted.

Archaeologists are itching to get their hands on the monastery and rip it down so they can see what the Harappans had underneath. "It is a third-rate architectural monument," grumbles Stuart Piggot, "and it is to be hoped that the site will be dealt with satisfactorily in the future." The Buddhists, understandably, feel differently, and the monastery remains and gives every indication of standing for a very long time.

The stark, utilitarian appearance of the residential section of Mohenjo-daro, and the lack of any obvious social or religious hierarchy, has given rise to some gloomy guesswork as to the kind of life lived by the Harappans. Says the archaeological writer Robert Silverberg: "The monotonous, communistic, barracks-like appearance of the city suggests that it may have been ruled by some faceless, anonymous committee, rather than by a king who reigned in splendor." Stuart Piggott is even more severe: "The secrecy of those blank brick walls, unadorned architecture of even the citadel buildings, the monotonous regularity of the streets, the stifling weight of dead tradition all combine to make the Harappa civilization one of the least attractive phases of ancient Oriental history . . . I can only say that there is something in the Harappa civilization that I find repellent." And Leonard Cottrell dubs it "1984—B.C." On the other hand, to Mortimer Wheeler, Mohenjo-daro in its prime "bespeaks middle-class prosperity with zealous municipal controls."

An ancient 1984, or a well-run model town—you may think what you like. Every way we turn, in an attempt to get some picture of the life of the obviously remarkable Harappans, we seem to run into that same blank featureless wall. They are the most frustrating people.

But they could write. In 1856 the railroad workers dug up lots of small stones, with pictures cut into them. Surrounding the pictures were little squiggly lines which might have been a design but which have since been identified as a system of pictographic writing. We call the writing the Indus valley script and it remains one of the great unread languages of the world. If philologists are confronted with an unknown language, but one which is set down in a familiar script, they have a chance at deciphering it. If they are given a known language, which is written in an unknown script, again they have a chance. But the Indus valley script is an unknown language, written in an unknown script. As far as experts have been able to determine, it is not related to any other written language. Many scholars have attempted the laborious task of deciphering the script. Some have even claimed they had succeeded, but they had not. Their translations turned out to be nonsense, as their colleagues gleefully pointed out. In 1932 there was more than the usual ripple of excitement when the Hungarian linguist Wilhelm von Hevesy announced that he had found an astounding similarity between the unread script of the Indus valley and the equally unread system of writing found on the *rongorongo* boards of Easter Island.

True enough, there seemed to be more than a coincidental relationship between the funny little figures contained in both writings. Some speculators had the Harappans trekking across Asia and sailing out into the Pacific. Today, however, few still believe the two systems are directly related. Neither von Hevesy nor anyone else has been able to do much with the supposed similarity. Both languages remain a mystery.

Even more discouraging is the realization that, barring some kind of spectacular and totally unexpected discovery, the Indus valley script will almost certainly remain unread for all time. Egyptian hieroglyphics were mysterious for years. But the Egyptians wrote profusely. They covered walls and rolls of papyrus with their intricate, beautiful hieroglyphics. Scholars could crack the Egyptian system of writing because they had so much raw material to work with. But the Harappans did not do a lot of writing, or if they did, the writing was done on a material that has decayed. Actually, it is hard to imagine how such a well-ordered society kept going without a profusion of written records. But the only examples of the Indus valley script that have come down to us are on the tiny seal stones, a few fragments of pottery and some scrawling on walls. These inscriptions rarely contain more than half a dozen characters—not much to work from. And even if they could be read, they would probably contain only the personal names of the owners of the seals or ritual inscriptions. There is no Harappan Homer here. Nor is there even a list of kings or important officials which might give the scholars some sort of framework upon which to construct a history of the peoples of the Indus.

The austere Harappans did not seem to go in for much bric-a-brac. Only eleven more or less fragmentary pieces of stone sculpture have been found at Mohenjo-daro, in addition to a few bronzes. But there is an abundance of terra-cotta figures. Most of the latter are crudely made, and one guesses they may have been children's toys, although archaeologists think they had a religious function.

From these bits of sculpture we get our only hint of what the Harappans looked like. One of the best-preserved pieces of stone sculpture is the bust of a man with a well-trimmed beard. The most unusual aspects of this face are the man's low receding forehead and his narrow, contemplative eyes. The lips are curved slightly in what appears to be a domineering sneer. This has led archaeologists to label the sculpture "priest-king," or "deity," but the label is only a convenience. No personality really emerges from this or other similar heads that have been found.

The same cannot be said for the small bronze figurine the archaeologists have called the dancing girl. She is naked except for a necklace and an armful of bangles. Both her pose and expression are at once arrogant and provocative. No mysteries here—she is the type of model that has been a favorite subject of artists down through the ages.

If these sculptures are representative of what the Harappans produced, the conclusion must be that they were not very distinguished artists. Or were they? There is a hint of something far greater in the field of art. At Harappa archaeologists found two small broken stone torsos that are so unique, so good, that scholars still hesitate to believe the Harappans made them.

John Marshall was aghast when they were shown to him. "When I first saw them, I found it difficult to believe that they were prehistoric; they seemed so completely to upset all established ideas about early art. Modeling such as this was unknown in the ancient world up to the Hellenistic age of Greece, and I thought, therefore, that some mistake must surely have been made; that the figures belonged to the Indo-Greek, Scythian or Parthian period in the Punjab, and somehow or other had found their way into levels some 3,000 years older than those to which they properly belonged. This too, I expect, will be the first idea of everyone else who is familiar with the history of early sculpture."

Marshall goes on to point out that the two torsos were unearthed by different men in different parts of the city. "Now it is possible, though the possibility is remote, that one of these two statuettes might at some time or other have worked its way down through 6 to 10 feet of ruined masonry and pottery into the older strata; but that two should have done this in different parts of the site, and that these two should be the only objects of a later age found under the layers of prehistoric debris, is well-nigh incredible."

Besides, Marshall points out, there are technical and stylistic differences between this and all other sculpture found in India. ". . . no parallel to this statue [one of the two torsos] is to be found among Indian sculptures of the historic period. Indeed, what we have to try and realize, not only about this but about the other statuette as well, is that, altogether apart from the circumstances of their finding, it is almost as difficult to account for them on the assumption that they belong to the historic as it is on the assumption that they belong to the prehistoric age."

So it is that the Harappans, who are always denounced for their faceless conformity, may actually have anticipated the naturalistic art forms of those most celebrated of all ancient individualists, the Greeks.

The statues are minor mysteries. The great mystery about the Indus civilization is: where did it come from? Quite suddenly, it seems, it is there, covering a thousand miles and more along the river. Its two great cities, probably the largest in the world at the time, are built, at once, on the same master plan.

This appearance of suddenness may simply be due to incomplete archaeology. The most promising places to look for remains of the development of Harappan civilization are the lowest levels of the mounds at Mohenjo-daro. Archaeologists have excavated many of the mounds down to the level of the present flood plain. From there on down the strata are drowned in ground water, and extremely difficult to work with. In 1956 archaeologists used a drill to dig up signs of human occupation some thirty-nine feet below the level of the plain—

an astonishing accumulation. So it seems that people had been living at Mohenjo-daro for a very long time.

But this does not mean that Harappan civilization developed slowly. On the contrary, Mortimer Wheeler believes that the Harappans had a rapid, almost explosive development. The Indus valley, he says, offered both a lure and a challenge to people.

"A society determined to profit by the vast opportunities [of the Indus valley] must have the genius and the skill to master an exacting and minatory environment, *and must have it from the outset*. A civilization such as that of the Indus cannot be visualized as a slow and patient growth. Its victories, like its problems, must have been of a sudden sort; and our search therefore for a systematic material ancestry for Indus civilization may well be a long and subtle and perhaps not primarily important one."

The people of the Indus, Wheeler points out, had an advantage: two other great civilizations, both built on the banks of rivers and both facing similar problems, had already developed, one in Mesopotamia and the other in Egypt. "In any physical sense, neither of these was the immediate parent; the Indus civilization, with its individual technology and script and its alien personality, was no mere colony of the West. But ideas have wings, and in the third millennium the idea of civilization was in the air of western Asia. A model of civilization, however abstract, was present to the minds of the Indus founders. In their running battle against more spacious problems than had been encountered either in Mesopotamia or in Egypt, they were fortified by the consciousness that it, or something like it, had been done before."

In 1946, on the basis of the best information available, Wheeler proposed that the Harappan civilization covered a period from 2500 to 1500 B.C., "without any emphasis on the exactitude of the terminal figures." Since that time the physicists have presented archaeologists with the tool of radiocarbon dating. The popular impression, that radiocarbon dating allows everything to be pinpointed, is wide of the mark. Writes Wheeler, perhaps displaying a bit of the old-time field archaeologists disdain for new-fangled "wonders": "At its best, in dealing with late prehistoric and early protohistoric cultures, we have to confess that radiocarbon analysis, a marvel for which we are properly grateful, is nevertheless a blunt instrument." Wheeler's original dates still stand.

Without radiocarbon analysis the best way of establishing the dates of an unknown civilization is to link it somehow with a civilization where the dates are known. The ubiquitous seal stones of the Harappans have turned up in ruins associated with the great empire builder of Mesopotamia, Sargon of Akkad. The dates of Sargon are established as well as any in ancient history as 2370 to 2344 B.C. So at that point, at least, there was some trade between the Indus and the land of Mesopotamia.

Sargon records that ships from Dilmun, Magan and Meluhha docked at his new capital, Agade. The location of these places is unknown, but the name Dilmun provides a hint. The Sumerians, who ruled the land of Mesopotamia before Sargon, wrote of Dilmun or Telmun, which they regarded as a worldly paradise similar to their own. This may indicate another civilization. Dilmun was a place "where the sun rises"—east of Sumer. Trade between Dilmun and Sumer was extensive. Ur-Nanshe of Lagash records the arrival of a shipment of timber from Dilmun about 2450 B.C. Other Sumerian tablets speak of shipments of precious objects from Meluhha.

Are Dilmun and Meluhha references to the Indus valley and its civilization? Some authorities think so.

There is one other scrap of evidence as to the proper naming of the Harappans. In the *Rig-Veda*, hymns of the Aryan conquerors, the conquered people are once referred to as the Mleccha. Can we overlook the similarity between Meluhha and Mleccha? This is the sort of identification game philologists play endlessly.

Both land and water routes between the Indus and Mesopotamia have been traced, and it is fairly safe to assume the two lands conducted an appreciable trade. The people of the Indus sent wood, gold and ivory, all mentioned in Mesopotamian records, and perhaps cotton. In return, they received . . . what? Although Indus products have been found in Mesopotamia, few Mesopotamian items have been found in the valley of the Indus. A guess is that the Mesopotamians sent cloth and other perishable goods.

A few Harappan items have been unearthed in other parts of the Near and Middle East, but trading was a secondary occupation for the Harappans. The basis of life on the Indus, as it was for all other early river civilizations, was agriculture.

Looking at the desolation of Mohenjo-daro now, it's hard to imagine that a flourishing city was surrounded by fields of wheat and barley, yet seeds from these plants are found among the ruins. One cannot forget that the building which occupied the most imposing site within the most important part of the city was the granary. In addition to the staple grain, there were peas, melons, sesame seeds and dates. The cultivation of cotton may have started with the Harappans, for the earliest traces of cotton known anywhere in the world have been found in the Indus cities.

The seal stones convey what is considered a fairly accurate

record of the Harappans' domestic animals. The most frequently shown is the humped cattle, still common in India today. Then there are dogs and cats, pigs, camels, horses and elephants. No one is sure if the elephant was domestic or wild, because the seals also abound with pictures of wild animals.

Harappan civilization was born, rapidly it seems, from the marshes of the Indus valley. Its influence spread over an enormous area, and the civilization continued without any major changes for a thousand years. Then these people, who seem to have evolved so perfect an order that no change was necessary, fell, apparently before the onslaught of barbarian invaders.

But when Indra and his Aryans overran Mohenjo-daro, it was no longer the well-built, compulsively orderly metropolis it had been in previous centuries. The old buildings had fallen to ruin, and atop them were piled haphazard jerry-built structures.

Floods, always a danger at Mohenjo-daro, seem to have become more frequent and severe in the city's later days. Overcutting of trees, overgrazing of land, and perhaps a change in the flow of the Indus itself may have destroyed the water supply system. Economic decline was the inevitable result. Wheeler speaks of Mohenjo-daro "steadily wearing out its landscape; alternatively . . . being steadily worn out by its landscape."

The once thriving trade with Mesopotamia seems to have become more complicated and less frequent. Harappan civilization was in decline. The decline did not proceed at a uniform rate throughout the entire area of Harappan influence, but some evidence of decline is reflected everywhere.

In recent years, some scientists have come to believe that catastrophic changes in the Indus, which caused flooding on an unprecedented scale, supplied the *coup de grâce* for the civilization. Others, like Mortimer Wheeler, hold out for the Aryan invasion. "This cannot be proved and may be quite incorrect, but it is not an impossibility."

Certainly the approximate date of the fall of Mohenjo-daro and the approximate date of the Aryan invasion fit well enough. If we discount the invasion and assume that all India had sunk into a liwly state, what explains those forts that Indra and his Aryan followers took such pride in destroying?

Finally, there is the evidence of the skeletons of Mohenjo-daro. In the anonymity of the city ruins these half-dozen groups of skeletons give dramatic proof that the brick-lined streets of Mohenjo-daro were once the scene of human tragedy. These groupings occur in the highest strata of the city ruins. It is probable, though not firmly established, that they all come from the same period, in fact that the individuals in all the groups met their deaths on the same day.

In one group there are fourteen skeletons of men and women and a child, surrounded by ornaments of the Harappan period. The confused and contorted positions of the skeletons suggest that death came violently. Two of the skulls bear the traces of ax or sword cuts.

Another group of nine contains five children. The excavation report notes that all are "in strangely contorted attitudes crowded together." The bodies may have been "thrown pell-mell into a hurriedly made pit." As some elephant tusks were found in the pit the excavators guessed the group may have been a family of ivory workers "who tried to escape with their belongings at the time of the raid but were stopped and slaughtered by the raiders," then disposed of in a shallow grave.

In total, more than thirty skeletons have been found, and

only nine, the presumed family of ivory workers, show any sign of having been buried at all. In the climate of Mohenjo-daro, bodies simply cannot be left lying about—decay begins too quickly. After the killings, the city must have been abandoned. Indeed, since a mere thirty skeletons were found, it is a fairly safe guess that the city was virtually uninhabited before the barbarians made their final raid to pick off the stragglers.

So there it is: Mohenjo-daro, the hill of the dead, is truly that. The most intensive archaeological investigation has had little success illuminating the kind of life which must have taken place within the brick city.

We can trace some elements in our lives today directly back to the people of Mesopotamia. The contributions of the Egyptians are well known. But what of the Harappans, whose civilization was far greater than that of either Mesopotamia or Egypt? Was their influence snuffed out completely? We can only guess. Certainly after the fall of the Harappans the cultural unity they imposed fragmented, and the whole Indus valley seems to have sunk back to a much lower level of material civilization.

But in Hinduism there are hints that the Aryan invaders of India picked up some non-Aryan ideas from the people they replaced. There is, for example, the Hindu reverence toward animals, particularly the bull. Animal figures are the most common element among the Harappan seals and terra-cotta statues, the bull being the dominant creature. Mortimer Wheeler has the final guess: "Paradoxically it would appear that the Indus civilization transmitted to its successors a metaphysics that endured, whilst it failed utterly to transmit the physical civilization which is its present monument."

There is a depressing footnote to the story of Mohenjo-daro. The ruins of the city are crumbling at an alarming rate. Wheeler estimates that unless dramatic steps are taken there will be nothing left in 20 years. The cost of saving Mohenjo-daro might run as high as $3.15 million. Pakistan hopes that a world-wide campaign, run by UNESCO, will raise the money for the site. But ancient sites all over the world are in peril, and money for such projects is thinly spread.

"If we can't save it, we shall just have to give it a decent burial," Wheeler has said.

SEVEN

THE KINGDOM OF
PRESTER JOHN

The Lost Christendom

Next to Atlantis the most eagerly sought-after legendary land was the one said to be ruled by a man who was both priest and king—the land of Prester John. Throughout the middle ages and well into that era that we have come to call the age of exploration, the belief persisted that out there, just beyond the borders of absolute geographical knowledge, existed a vast and wonderful Christian kingdom.

At first this kingdom was supposed to have been in India. But when the Christians got to India and found no Prester John, they simply assumed his kingdom existed farther to the east. When the entire continent of Asia was eliminated, the quest was then transferred to Africa.

The legend of the kingdom of Prester John persisted, in spite of all evidence to the contrary, because it served an important function. During some of the darkest hours in European history, Christians could console themselves with the thought that at any moment the hosts of the Priest-King might come pouring out from the East to save them.

One such story of salvation from the East reached Europe in 1221. There was a report that a mysterious Christian monarch was inflicting great slaughter on the Moslems of Central Asia. It was rumored that this Christian conqueror was on the point of marching westward to relieve the Crusaders, still clinging precariously to parts of the Holy Land. Perhaps he would even appear in Europe.

The information had come from unimpeachable sources. Two prominent churchmen, Jacquis de Vity, Bishop of Acre, and Cardinal Pelagius, both influential men in the army of the Crusaders, had sent accounts of the conqueror in letters from the Holy Land. Both men called the monarch King David. One thought he was the son or grandson of Prester John; the other believed he was the fabulous Priest-King himself.

Only slowly and very reluctantly did Europe wake up to the fact that this report from the Orient was only half correct. Someone was slaughtering Moslems and everyone else in Central Asia, but this conqueror was no Christian King David or Prester John—he was Genghis Khan. Even after the identification was made, the fantasy would not die completely. Europeans continued to insist that Genghis Khan and his Mongols really were Christians. This was not the first time a story of the coming of Prester John disappointed Europe, and it would not be the last.

The Pope wrote to Prester John; Marco Polo looked for him, and so did Prince Henry the Navigator. Vasco da Gama even thought he had found Prester John's kingdom. His name was on everyone's lips; the people knew of his kingdom with all its wonders. Prester John was more famous and certainly more popular with the common folk of Europe than any European ruler.

As far as we can trace it, the story began in Rome in the year 1122, with a mysterious visitor from the East. Two early documents record that in that year a man calling himself "John Patriarch of the Indians" or simply "an archbishop of India" came to Rome to see Pope Calixtus II. This John said that his journey from India had taken a year.

Patriarch John remained in Rome another year, and during his stay he entertained his follow churchmen with descriptions of India. Particularly wonderful were the stories he told of the Shrine of St. Thomas. Western churchmen didn't know much about St. Thomas, except that he was one of the original apostles of Christ and that after the crucifixion he had traveled east to India to preach the gospel. The stories of the conversions he made there and of his ultimate martyrdom could be found only in documents of doubtful authority. Yet here was a man from the very Christian community St. Thomas himself had founded. The Saint, Patriarch John told them, was well remembered in India, and his tomb was a magnificent monument to which pilgrims flocked, where they could witness miracles performed almost daily.

After Patriarch John departed from Rome, he disappeared into the same obscurity from which he had come. There is no record that he ever mentioned the name of Prester John during his stay, but many of the wonders he spoke of were soon to be attributed to that king.

Some of the more sophisticated and worldly among the Roman clergy might well have been suspicious of the strange man from India. They had never heard of a large Christian community in India, and for a very good reason—there was none. Patriarch John was an impostor.

In 1145 another wanderer from the East arrived at the Papal court. This time the traveler was no imposter; he was Bishop Hugh of Jabala, a small coastal town in Syria near Antioch. The year before, the area of Jabala had been overrun by Moslems, and Bishop Hugh had traveled to Rome to appeal to the reigning Pope, Eugenius III, for aid. While at Rome he met Bishop Otto of Freising, a noted historian of the day. Naturally Bishop Otto was anxious to learn all he could of conditions in Syria and the East. From his conversations with the Syrian churchman, Bishop Otto recorded the following:

"He [Bishop Hugh] related also that many years before a certain John, a king and priest who dwells beyond Persia and Armenia in the uttermost East and, with all his people, is a Christian but a Nestorian, made war upon his brother kings of Persians and Medes . . . Prester John, for so they accustomed to call him, putting the Persians to flight." After this victory, Prester John ". . . advanced to fight for the Church at Jerusalem; but when he arrived at the Tigris and lacking a means of transportation for his army, he turned northward, as he had heard that the river in that quarter was frozen over in winter. After halting on its banks for some years in expectation of frost he was obliged to return home."

Bishop Hugh also added these details: "It is said that he [Prester John] is a lineal descendant of the Magi, of whom mention is made in the Gospel, and that ruling over the same peoples which they governed he enjoys such great glory and wealth that he uses no scepter save one of emerald . . . Inflamed by the example of his fathers who came to adore Christ in his manager, he had planned to go to Jerusalem . . ."

Bishop Hugh made the same mistake that the Bishop of Acre and Cardinal Pelagius were to make some eighty years later: he confused a nomadic conqueror with the Christian Prester John. In 1141, the time of Prester John's reported defeat of the "Persians and Medes" in Central Asia, the Moslems of central Asia had suffered a stunning defeat at the hands of Yeh-lu Ta-shish, ruler of the empire of Qarakhitay or Black Cathay. The decisive battle took place near Samarkand (in what is now Soviet Central Asia), when the nomad armies routed those of Seljuk Sultan Sanjar.

Even after the proper identification was made, those who had originally believed in Prester John still could not reconcile themselves to the idea that this was entirely a case of mistaken identity. Yeh-lu Ta-shish, they insisted, was a Christian. But he was not. He was a Chinese-educated Buddhist. He led a seminomadic conglomeration of nations, which doubtless included some persons who professed the Nestorian Christian faith. Most nomads were casual or indifferent about their religion and by no stretch of the imagination can the empire of Black Cathay be identified as the land of Prester John.

Communications from places like Samarkand were infrequent and unreliable. News of Yeh-lu Ta-shish's defeat of the Seljuk Sultan was carried two thousand miles from Central Asia, to Jabala on the Syrian coast, by wandering merchants, many of them Nestorians. Somewhere on the journey one of them inserted the name of Prester John in place of that of the nomad. Christians had no quarrels with Buddhists; they barely knew Buddhists existed. The great struggle throughout the world that they knew was between Christians and Moslems. If someone had defeated the Moslems, it followed that he must be a Christian, and if he was a Christian from the East, then he must be Prester John himself.

The kingdom of Prester John was known in Europe in

the 1140s but it did not become famous until 1165. In that year the Eastern Roman Emperor at Constantinople, Manuel I, received a long, poorly printed but exceedingly arrogant and fascinating letter from a man who signed himself "Presbyter Johannes, by the power and virtue of God and of the Lord Jesus Christ, Lord of Lords." This document came to be known simply as "the Letter."

Despite the decline of the Eastern Roman Empire, Manuel I was still regarded as the most powerful Christian monarch in the world. Yet John's tone was almost scornful:

"If Thou, Manuel, wilt discern My greatness and My excellence and if Thou wilt know where upon earth Our omnipotence reigneth, Thou shall admit and believe without doubting that I, Prester John, am the Lord of Lords and that I surpass all the kings of the whole earth in riches, mercy and omnipotence. Seventy-two kings pay tribute to Us alone."

Page after page Prester John continued extolling the wonders of his realm and his own power and Christian virtue: "If Thou canst count the stars of the sky and the sands of the sea judge the vastness of Our realm and Our power."

One oddity was this great king's humble title of prester or priest—John the Priest-King. Often he was called simply the Priest. The Letter explains this modesty:

"Wherefore it will not astonish Thy sagacity that Our venerable person may not be named by worthier name than that of Prester. We have at Our court many ministers possessing higher spiritual offices and dignities. Our Lord High Steward, for example, is a Primate and King, Our cupbearer a King and Archbishop, Our Chamberlain a Bishop and King, Our Marshal a King and Archimandrite, Our Master of Our Kitchens a King and Abbot. And therefore it doth not beseem Our Highness to be named by the same names and bear the same ranks as those with which Our palace overflows. Our Eminence therefore prefers out of humility to be designated with a lesser name and office."

Manuel forwarded the astonishing document to Frederick Barbarosa, the Holy Roman Emperor. Another copy was brought to the attention of Pope Alexander III. Of the three leading figures of Christendom, only the Pope replied to the Letter. At least we think he replied. There is a rather strange document attributed to Alexander III and dated September 27, 1177, some twelve years after the original Prester John letter made its appearance in Europe. The Pope's letter is not addressed to Prester John and never mentions that name or any other. But most authorities have assumed that since it is written to a distant, powerful and extremely arrogant Christian monarch, it can be meant for none other than the Priest-King.

Pope Alexander indicates that he knows a good deal about this foreign monarch. He recites how he has already heard from various persons about the piety and good works of the monarch. But the Pope warns, "The more magnanimously thou conductest thyself, and the less thou vauntest of thy wealth and power, the more readily shall we regard thy wishes both as to the concession of a church in the city and of altars in the church of SS. Peter and Paul and in the church of the Lord's supper at Jerusalem, and as to another reasonable requests . . ."

The requests for churches and altars in Rome and Jerusalem were not contained in the original Prester John letter. They were apparently communicated directly to the Pope by his own personal physician, Philip, who had "contacts with many persons in the East." And it was to Philip that the Pope gave his reply, in the hope that the physician would carry it back to the representatives of the mysterious monarch. Philip himself is a mystery. We don't know who he was or where in the East he had been or what he did with the Pope's letter after it was given to him. He simply drops out of history.

After the Pope's letter, no other person of importance seems to have attempted to open a correspondence with Prester John. But the Letter itself became enormously popular and was translated into every European language. It appeared in many versions, each one vying with the next in the enumeration of the wonder of Prester John's kingdom.

The reason for the Letter's popularity is easy enough to understand. For the medieval European stuck in the humdrum of everyday life, and with little real knowledge of the outside world, the Letter made exciting reading. A German version contains this account of some of the creatures of Prester John's land:

"For there are also very many wild people who have horns on their heads and do not know any language; they yelp and grunt like pigs. There are also many sidicus in the same region, which fly to the people in the fields and speak to them and greet them with proper speech, as though they spoke the tongue of men. Priest John also has mountains of gold and other metal; there mice and ants and other animals dig out the gold, so that it is found beautiful and pure, which is not such hard work as here in our country . . ."

The parts about the horned men and gold-digging mice and ants are fables, but the account of the sidicus is not. This marvelous creature is described in greater detail elsewhere in the Letter:

". . . there too is found the sidicus which is a beautiful kind of bird. And it understands human speech: these birds talk to one another and answer correctly like humans, so learned are they. . . The bird is green all over its body, save only its feet and its beak which are red; and the bird has a long tail and has a red band round its neck and has a tongue like that of a man and is long and thin, not much bigger than a woodpecker."

Fanciful and exaggerated, but still a serviceable description of a parrot. The parrot was unkown in Europe at that time, and the first tales of it must have been brought back by the Crusaders. That is typical of the Letter. It was a virtual compilation of all the fabulous stories ever told about India and "the uttermost East," with a few authentic bits of information scattered throughout.

Many of the fabulous events related in the Letter seem to have come from the same source as the tales of St. Thomas, that the false Patriarch John had told in Rome in 1122. Indeed, the stories of St. Thomas and those of Prester John became so thoroughly intermingled that the medieval European often confused the two.

The circumstances through which the Prester John letter was introduced into Europe are unclear. The first known copies of the Letter were written in Latin and appeared around 1165. But they contain a note that they are a translation made by the Archbishop of Mainz from the Greek original. But no early Greek copy of the Letter has yet turned up, and most scholars think that the Letter was first written in Latin, and the business about the Greek translation was simply tacked on to make it sound more authentically Eastern. The German archbishop seems to have had nothing to do with it.

The Prester John letter was an obvious literary concoction. Every bit of knowledge, legendary or real, that a well-read European might have was crammed into this document. It made the East sound like the world of Sinbad the Sailor (in fact some of the details were probably drawn from Sinbad stories). It read just like a species of romantic literature that was becoming increasingly popular in Europe—indeed that is just what it was—but it had come at the right moment. Europe was looking for good news from the East. The Second Crusade, launched in 1147, had been little short of a disaster. The Crusaders' Christian states in the Holy Land were again harassed by the Moslems, who had reorganized after their defeats during the First Crusade. Even the Christians of Europe, particularly those of Eastern Europe, began to feel the threat of Islam. Suddenly here was word that a fabulously powerful Christian king was ready to take the Moslems from behind. Just how seriously the Letter was taken is impossible to say. But whether they believed the details or not, the people of medieval Europe knew of the land of Prester John and were convinced that it existed somewhere. They continued firm in this belief even after the disappointing confusion of Genghis Khan and Prester John in 1221.

Although the Mongols did not turn out to be Christians, they were not Moslems either. Mongol domination of Asia brought a terrified stability to that continent and gave Europeans the chance to travel eastward that the sultans had denied them. Men like Plano Carpini, Simon of St. Quentin and William Rubruck all made the arduous journey from Europe to Asia. All hoped and expected to find the kingdom of Prester John.

Marco Polo too had searched for the land of the Priest-King. But when he returned to Venice in 1295 after nearly a quarter of a century of travel in Asia, he had very little to tell his countrymen about Prester John. Marco had seen the wonders of the court of Kublai Kahn, but nothing of the

Christian marvels of the land of Prester John. Naturally, the Venetians, who knew that Prester John existed, but were not all sure about Kublai Kahn, thought Marco was a liar.

Marco did, however, report one interesting bit of gossip he had picked up in the East about Prester John. He said there had been an "Unc Khan," alias Prester John, who had been a Christian lord of the Tatars until defeated by Genghis Khan. Other travelers also picked up word of this Christian "Tatar." He was known variously as Ung Khan, Wang Khan or King John. Not only the Europeans but the Mongols themselves have left records of this ruler.

So it seems that there really was an important Christian ruler in Central Asia during the early middle ages. He was a king of the Kereits, a people the Oriental scholar René Grousset has described as "one of the most mysterious peoples in history."

Grousset writes: "They were by origin Turco-Mongol— so much is sure. But how far predominantly one or the other we have no means of telling. They make to all intents and purposes their first appearance in the chronicles only in the generation before Chingis-Khan [Genghis Khan], and step forthwith into a leading role."

Both Christian and Mongol sources agree the Kereits were Christian. Says Grousset: "If we are to believe the Syrian chronicler Bar Hebraeus, they were converted shortly after the year 1000. One of their kings had got lost in the desert. At his last gasp, he was saved by the miraculous appearance of Saint Sergius. Touched by grace, and at the instigation of Christian merchants then passing through his kingdom, he sent to the Nestorian Metropolitan of Merv, in Khorassan, Ebed-jesu, with a request that priests should come to baptize himself and his people. A letter from Ebed-jesu to the Nestorian Patriarch of Baghdad, John VI, dated 1100 and quoted by Bar Hebraeus, states that nomads were then baptized with their king to the number of 200,000."

How much truth there is in this story is impossible to determine, but it is definitely established that by the twelfth century there was a powerful Kereit Christian kingdom of the steppe. But the king in whom we are interested, Ung or Wang Khan, was more of a typical nomad chief than he was a model for the Christian Prester John. Wang Khan gained his throne in the usual way, by murdering several of his brothers and their families. He maintained his power through clever alliances with other tirbes, and through more than the usual amount of treachery and brutality against friends and enemies alike.

This nomad leader is usually called Wang Khan, as though that were his name. It is not, it is a title, and he should really be called the Wang Khan. His proper name was Toghril. Wang Khan is a strange title since it essentially means "king king." Khan was the nomad's title for king or leader. Wang was a Chinese word for king. Toghril was awarded the title of Wang by the Chinese, but he also retained his old title of Khan. The Mongols wrote the word Wang as Ung, and so to the Mongols, who recorded most of the details of this ruler's life, he was the Ung Khan. When Marco Polo heard the name he got confused and called him Unc Khan. The similarity in pronuciation between Khan and John was too much for the European Christians to overlook.

One of the men to have sought the protection of the powerful Wang Khan was a young Mongol, of noble lineage but unfortunate circumstances. His name was Temüjin, later to be known by his title, Genghis Khan. The young Genghis

Khan and the Wang Khan were allies, if not friends, for many years. When Genghis Khan's power had grown great enough to challenge his old protector, he did so successfully, and destroyed the Christian empire of the steppe. However, Genghis Khan and his descendants were to retain a rather warm feeling toward Christianity, and it became one of the several official religions of the Mongol Empire.

Although Marco Polo tentatively identified this Kereit king with Prester John, this is not how the legend got started. Stories of Prester John had reached Europe long before the Wang Khan was born, and they probably had been in circulation before the Kereits themselves were converted. The idea of Prester John was in the air, and it had simply been attached to a convenient figure.

Other shadowy accounts of Prester John or his descendants began to filter out of Central Asia, but the more travelers that went, the less they seemed to be able to find out about the lost kingdom. The land of Prester John was still pictured on maps, but his popularity in Europe was waning. Then in the fourteenth century a Dominican friar named Jordanus de Severac had an inspiration. Since Prester John obviously did not live in Central Asia, which by that time had been pretty well explored, then he must live in Central Africa, which had hardly been explored at all. Jordanus' reassignment gave the story of the Priest-King a new life.

No one knows why Jordanus decided to change Prester John's location. The change seems arbitrary to us, but it would not have seemed so to a man of the fourteenth century. Asia and Africa were regarded as part of the same continent, the dividing line between them being the Nile River. Prester John had simply retired to the African side of his vast domains after being driven out of the Asian side by Genghis Khan.

Besides, there really was a genuinely mysterious Christian kingdom flourishing in the middle of Africa, one far more substantial than the Nestorian empire of the Kereits. This was the kingdom of Abyssinia or Ethiopia. The Ethiopians like to trace their monotheistic heritage all the way back to Solomon and Sheba's son Menelik. But it is more probable that they remained pagans until converted to Christianity in the fourth century. The Ethiopian church was always schismatic, and the rise of Moslem power in Africa during the seventh century isolated the Ethiopian Christians from the rest of the Christian world. By the fourteenth century Europeans knew less about the Ethiopians than they did about the Mongols.

Fabulous stories had long circulated about Ethiopia. In the ninth century, for example, a Jew appeared in North Africa with a wonderful tale about "the Sons of Moses" who ruled a kingdom consisting of four of the Ten Lost Tribes of Israel. This kingdom, the storyteller said, was located somewhere beyond "the rivers of Ethiopia."

The search for the kingdom of Prester John in Africa continued well into the fifteenth century. Prince Henry the Navigator (1394–1460), the man who really inspired the Portuguese voyages to Africa and Asia, instructed his captains to try to find the lost land of the Christian king. When Vasco da Gama's ships landed at Mozambique he recorded in his logbook, "We were told that Prester John resided not far from this place; that he held many cities along the coast and the inhabitants of these cities were great merchants and owned big ships." Da Gama had probably picked up rumors of the inland empire of the Monomotapa, builder of Zimbabwe, but since the Prester John legend was so thoroughly believed, reports of any unknown empire in Africa were immediately identified with that of the great king of a lost Christendom.

For decades, maps of Africa continued to refer to Ethiopia as the land of Prester John. The first European book ever written on Ethiopia which appeared in the fifteenth century referred to the king of that land as Prester John or simply "the Preste."

Some modern scholars believe that despite its late identification as the land of Prester John, the legend itself really did refer to Ethiopia. They point out that one of the Ethiopian royal titles was *zan*, a word easily confused with John. The Ethiopian monarchs, incidentally, were insulted by this identification and proudly pointed out that they possessed a whole string of titles far more exalted than that of priest.

A refinement of this theory is that no matter where the Prester John legend itself originated, when Pope Alexander wrote the Priest-King in 1177 he was in reality addressing the king of Ethiopia. The Pope's letter specifically mentions his envoy had met with "honourable persons of the monarch's kingdom." These "honourable persons," the reasoning goes, "must have been the representatives of some real power, and not a phantom. It must have been a real king who professed to desire reconciliation with the Catholic Church and the assignation of a church at Rome and an altar at Jerusalem."

Whatever the truth of this theory may be, it finally became obvious to Europeans that the Prester John they sought did not reside in Ethiopia, or any other part of Africa, or anywhere else. The land of Prester John was and had always been legendary. A nagging question remains: how and where did this widely believed, and extraordinarily influential legend begin?

The most obvious answer is that the legend began when Bishop Hugh or some other Eastern Christian confused Yeh-lu Ta-shish with a Christian king simply because he was killing Moslems. Wrote one recent commentator, "Prester John, that king of rubies and diamonds, was tracked to a Mongol tent in a grim steppe."

But this identification does not really work. The idea of Prester John must have existed in Asia long before Yeh-lu Ta-shish, for the confusion to have occured, and it must have continued to exist independently of him so that it could become mixed with the exploits of other nomad conquerors. Then, too, there is no indication that the writer of the famous Prester John letter had ever heard of Yeh-lu Ta-shish or of Bishop Hugh's story of Prester John. He seems to have drawn his ideas of Prester John from some source besides the exploits of a nomad.

In the attempt to find the origin of the legends of the land of the Priest-King John, a great deal of scholarly detective work has been expended on trying to pinpoint the individual who fabricated the Prester John letter. Scholars have been able to trace most of the information to books that circulated in Western Europe at the time the Letter was written. But this document also contains some bits of information about the East that a Western European could not have obtained just by sitting around reading books.

The Letter speaks of a Patriarch of Samarkand and of "the Patriarch of St. Thomas." These were titles known in the East, but unknown in the West. One discordant note in the Letter is that Prester John says his kingdom is poor in horses. It seems the only shortcoming of an otherwise perfect land. As a matter of fact, India was known, in the East, for the poor quality of its horses. A Western European merely attempting to pile wonder upon wonder would hardly have included such an odd bit.

Vsevolod Slessarev, who did the most recent scholarly reexamination of the entire history of the Priest-King in his *Prester John, the Letter and the Legend,* concludes that the Letter was written by a twelfth-century Western European who apparently spent time in the East, probably with the Crusaders in the Holy Land.

There has been a good deal of speculation on why the unknown author of the Letter wrote it at all. One school of thought holds that it was a utopian manifesto, and a political document which exposed ideas of "natural democracy" to a wide audience. The thinking of this school is summed up by Paul Herrmann in the book *Conquest by Man:*

"The contrast between conditions in Europe and those in the ideal state of Prester John were glaring. Whereas the medieval emperors continued to have themselves designated and served as divine, the incomparably more powerful priest king declared that he was and remained a mortal man and was content, despite his almost divine omnipotence, to be a simple priest. And whereas the nascent monetary economy in Europe was beginning to make the 'God-given' antithesis between noble and burgher on the one hand and the oppressed peasant and disenfranchised day-labourer on the other painfully evident, the Christian Communist author of Prester John's letter laid emphasis on the fact that in the immeasurably wide and wealthy Eastern wonderland there was no private property, because everything belonged to God and his king priest. And finally whereas war, faction, dissension, envy, murder and violence were rampant in twelfth-century Europe, the lands of Prester John lived in a state of perpetual peace and tranquility, safe-guarded by law and free from all fear save that of Almighty God."

Slessarev brushes aside such theorizing and attributes no high and mighty aims to the author of the Letter. "If he had any ulterior motive outside his evident urge to compose a modest piece of literature, it may have been a desire to bolster the morale of the Crusaders by letting them hope for the imminent arrival of a mighty ally."

The first account of Prester John, that of Bishop Hugh, contains, in Slessarev's opinion, "a curious split on Prester John's personality. In a purely historical perspective he has to be equated with a Buddhist ruler of a Central Asian State while his legendary attributes tie him to St. Thomas and India."

Slessarev believes that the reason the Prester John story kept popping up from so many sources in the East, and for so many different reasons, is that the Priest-King was probably part of an ancient Nestorian legend, one of a cycle of legends which collected around the life of St. Thomas, the most important Christian figure connected with the Orient.

Nestorian Christianity takes its name from Nestorius, the patriarch of Constantinople from 428 to 431. Nestorian missionaries, burning with evangelical zeal, headed eastward founding Christian communities from Syria to China. Nestorian prelates and merchants of the Nestorian faith could be found in the camps of Mongol khans and in the sophisticated cities of China. Unlike the Western Christians, who were locked in a death struggle with the Moslems, the Nestorians were often able successfully to work out accommodations with Islamic peoples.

Although they lack any hard evidence to support the claim, the Nestorians themselves trace their foundations back to St. Thomas, the apostle who went to India. The only source for the deeds of St. Thomas in India is an apocryphal tract, *Acts of St. Thomas*, written in the third or fourth century. *Acts* has the Saint traveling to the northwest part of India, making many converts and performing many miracles before being martyred by Misdaeus, King of India. Later the king himself was stricken with repentance and converted. The Saint's body was placed in a magnificent tomb, and pilgrims who flocked to it witnessed all manner of miracles.

How much historical fact underlies these stories of St. Thomas is unknown. At one time it was believed that the stories were entirely legendary. But then scholars were able to identify one of the Indian kings mentioned in *Acts* as a real king. This isn't much to go on, but scholars now treat *Acts* with a little more respect.

Whatever real successes St. Thomas may have had in India, Christianity certainly did not survive there. But the stories of the wonders the Saint had performed were kept alive and circulated throughout the widely scattered Nestorian communities. Occasionally, they even penetrated into the Roman Catholic world of Western Europe.

The theory that Prester John originated in a Nestorian myth was first proposed by Alexander von Humboldt, the great traveler and natural scientist. Slessarev picks up this idea and attempts to pinpoint the exact myth.

The king who ordered St. Thomas' death but later converted in repentance had a son named Vizan. In the rewriting of the story this name has often been changed to John. Vizan-John might have become the successor not only to his father's royal title, but also to St. Thomas' position as leader of the Indian Christians as well. St. Thomas was to have gone to northwest India, but there were no Christians there when the legend of Prester John began to circulate. The nearest major Christian community was at Samarkand in the steppes—hence the easy confusion between the Mongol khans who battled at Samarkand and the legendary Priest-King.

Unfortunately the existence of a Nestorian Prester John legend is unproven. The great Nestorian library at Edessa was destroyed by the Moslems, and with it went the bulk of Nestorian literature. The faith itself was severely weakened by the Tatar conqueror Tamerlane in the fourteenth century and today is almost extinct. But there are still many Nestorian documents that rest untranslated and unread in archives and libraries throughout the Orient. Perhaps in one of them the elusive Priest-King will finally be traced to his home.

If such legend indeed existed, all the missing pieces of the Prester John puzzle would fall into place. We can see the anonymous writer of the Prester John letter hearing of the Nestorian Vizan-John while with the Crusaders. Using the scanty legend as a skeleton, he fills it out by adding everything else he knows or has heard about India and the mysterious East.

Says Slessarev: "The author took these authentic bits of legend, surrounded them with a profusion of arbitrarily picked up material on India, and with them surprised the world!"

EIGHT

ZIMBABWE

The Place of Stones

Duarte Barbosa was one of the more perceptive of the Portuguese adventurers who came to Africa at the beginning of the sixteenth century. During his stay in the coastal town of Sofala in Mozambique in 1517, Barbosa listened to the stories of Arab traders who had visited all parts of the vast continent.

"Beyond this country toward the interior lies the great kingdom of Benametapa pertaining to the heathen whom the Moors call Kaffirs: they are black men and go naked save from the waist down," wrote Barbosa.

There were rumors of any number of inland kingdoms, but the "kingdom of Benametapa" was considered the most powerful. Continued Barbosa: "Fifteen or twenty days' journey inland is a great town called Zimbaoche, . . . the king of Benametapa often stays there . . . In this town of Benametapa is the king's most usual abode, in a very large building, and thence the traders carry the inland gold to Sofala and give it unweighed to the Moors for colored cloths and beads, which are greatly esteemed among them."

Occasionally men from this inland kingdom would come to Sofala. Barbosa describes the noblemen as wearing skin robes which trailed on the ground and carrying "swords thrust into wooden scabbards, bound with much gold and other metals . . . They also carry assegais [spears] in their hands, and others carry bows and arrows of middle size . . . The iron arrowheads are long and finely pointed. They are warlike men, and some too are great traders."

A few years later Damião de Goes, another early Portuguese voyager to Africa, wrote, "In the middle of this country is a fortress built of large and heavy stones inside and out. In other districts of the said plain there are other fortresses built in the same manner, in all of which the king has captains . . . The king of Benametapa keeps great state, and is served on bended knees with great reverence."

Writing at about the same time as de Goes, João de Barros, treasurer of Portugal's African colonies, began propagating the legends that have surrounded the African fortress of Zimbabwe for so many centuries. De Barros states that some believe the building to be the work of the devil, "since in view of their merely human strength and their ignorance, it is not possible that these buildings could have been built by the Blacks."

As far as we know neither de Barros, nor any other early Portuguese, ever actually saw the buildings of Zimbabwe. What they reported was hearsay. "In the opinion of the Arab who has seen the biuldings," de Barros continued, "they are very ancient and were erected there in order to guard the mines, which are also very ancient and from which no gold has been taken for a very long time, because of the upheavals of warfare."

Thus in the sixteenth century de Barros had laid out the three principal elements of the Zimbabwe legend: (1) The fortress could not possibly have been built by black Africans; (2) It was very ancient; (3) It had something to do with gold.

After these early Portuguese reports, a long silence fell upon Zimbabwe as far as European records are concerned. It is possible that an occasional European wanderer came across the site, but if he did, the records of his visit has been lost. African and Arab traders visited regularly but left no written accounts. The first white man we actually know of who saw Zimbabwe was Adam Renders, a German-American trader and ivory hunter. He was a strange sort of man. A scandal had forced him to abandon his family and to plunge deeply into Africa. The life suited him, and he ultimately married the daughter of one of the native chiefs. Renders went to Zimbabwe in 1868. It was deserted by then and he was unimpressed.

In 1871 an even stranger white man came stalking into the area of Zimbabwe. Karl Gottlieb Mauch was a thirty-four-year-old self-educated German geologist with the constitution of an elephant and the romantic inclinations of a poet. He had come to Africa to establish himself as a great explorer. Mauch could not afford and did not desire an elaborate expedition party. Wearing a leather suit of his own design, and festooned with sixty pounds of books and equipment, the sturdy red-bearded Mauch landed in South Africa and began walking. For six years he tramped the southern tip of the African continent. During his wanderings, he discovered several rich gold fields. He reported them but made no attempt to exploit them himself. Mauch wanted to be an explorer, not a gold hunter.

During the first years of his adventure, Mauch enjoyed extraordinary luck, but by 1871 it had run out. He had reached Mashonaland, that part of the southern end of Rhodesia which borders Mozambique. Half-starved, and without any resources at all, Mauch was imprisoned by a local chief, who intended to hold him for ransom. It looked like the end of the German's quixotic journey. Then, another white man turned up to pay the ransom. Incredibly enough, he also spoke German. The man was Adam Renders.

After this narrow escape and with his health broken, Mauch was thinking seriously of returning to Europe. But he had one more adventure in mind. Mauch had heard rumors that somewhere in the district there existed the ruins of the capital of a mighty soverign who had been called the Monomotapa. Did Renders know anything about the ruins? The helpful Renders said that not only had he heard of the ruins, but that he had actually camped there several times during the past few years.

Mauch got another piece of good news. An old friend of his, George Philips, an ivory hunter, was camped in the vicinity. Mauch sent for Philips, and along with Renders they headed for Zimbabwe. On September 5, 1871, Mauch climbed a hill and for the first time looked down upon the ruins of Zimbabwe, or at least as much of them as was visible through a blanket of vegetation.

He spent several days wandering about the walls and towers, exploring and mapping them. Most of the natives of the area avoided the ruins, and either knew nothing of their history, or would say nothing. However, he encountered an old man named Babareke, who claimed to be the son of the last "high priest" of Zimbabwe. From him Mauch obtained a strange story of religious rites which sounded to the German's ears like a description of the rites of the ancient Hebrews.

The following May, Mauch set out on his long journey home. He walked an exhausting 563 miles to the city of Sena in Mozambique. There he took a river boat down the Zambezi to the coast, and was able to find a ship captain willing to take an ill and penniless adventurer back to Europe. A few years later Karl Mauch met a prosaic end when he fell from the window of his house in Germany and died.

Before his death, however, Mauch made Zimbabwe famous by publishing a book containing his observations and speculations on its origins. Since that time this collection of stone buldings in the interior of Africa has tantalized the world.

What is Zimbabwe?

Actually, there are many Zimbabwes. De Barros had written, "the natives of the country call all these edifices Symbaoe, which according to their language signifies court, for every place where Benametapa may be is so called; and they say that being royal property all the king's other dwellings have this name . . ."

The name Symbaoe went through a number of changes until the spelling Zimbabwe was finally generally accepted. It means place of stones. More than three hundred roughly similar roofless stone structures have been found scattered over the Rhodesian plain. Some bear names like Little Zimbabwe or Clay Zimbabwe, but the one around which so many fantasies cluster is Great Zimbabwe.

Great Zimbabwe was built in the valley of the Mapudzi River in Mashonaland (now part of Rhodesia). It is a broad rolling valley rimmed by mountains and cliffs. Often the valley is broken by granite hillocks, some steep-sided and fantastically shaped. It is on one of these steep hills that the Zimbabwe ruins are located. From there they spread into the valley below covering over a quarter of a square mile.

Atop the hill, overlooking a ninety-foot precipice, is a walled complex of enclosures and narrow passages called the Acropolis. Natural outcrops and boulders have been incorporated into these walls by the builders. Almost everyone agrees that this structure, which is reachable only by a few narrow and winding passages, was a defensive stronghold.

No such agreement has been reached about the use of the other major structure at Zimbabwe. It is often called the Temple, although there is no particular reason to believe that's what it was. Its other name, "the Elliptical Building," is less controversial because the walls are roughly elliptical in shape. It stands on a lower hill about a quarter of a mile away from the Acropolis. The wall encloses an area some 350 feet across at its widest point. Within the massive main wall are a multitude of smaller walls, one of which runs parallel to the main wall for 220 feet to form what we now call the Parallel Passage.

Also within the Elliptical Building is the Conical Tower. This thirty-four-foot-high rounded tower has stimulated much unproven theorizing about phallic symbolism. A second smaller tower once stood nearby but has now been almost entirely ruined.

Between the main structures are the Valley Ruins, a less imposing set of buildings which seems to reproduce in miniature the features found in the major buildings.

Everything at Zimbabwe is dry masonry. Walls and towers were raised by carefully piling one layer of flat stones atop another, without any mortar. Dry masonry is a simple building technique and has been used in many places, but at Zimbabwe it was used extraordinarily well. Walls lean inward, and are curved to give them greater strength, so that they have survived the ravages of weather and creeping vegetation better than might be expected.

The building technique must have been suggested to the builders of Zimbabwe by the nature of their land. The rock of the river valley is granite, which splits off from cliffs and boulders in layers. These can easily be cut and shaped into the bricks that make up the buildings and walls.

The larger walls vary from twenty to thirty-three feet in height, and may be as wide as fifteen feet at the base, narrowing to ten feet near the top. The stones of the top of the main wall of the Elliptical Building are laid in a double chevron pattern, the only ornamentation that remains at Zimbabwe.

The Portuguese chronicler Damião de Goes, recording the descriptions of sixteenth-century Arab merchants, said it was "a fortress built of huge heavy stones. It is a strange close-joined building which looks the same inside as outside, since the stones are fitted together without mortar and are not painted. In the stone above the entrance is a carved inscription so old that no one knows how to read it."

Thus in the sixteenth century, when "The King of Benametapa" still held court at Zimbabwe, it looked essentially as it does today, except for that old inscription. De Goes' reference to an inscription has led to no end of excited speculation. Today most authorities agree that the inscription never existed and that the story started with a garbled description of the chevron pattern.

Today the Great Zimbabwe ruins are a Rhodesian national park. A good road leads from the city of Fort Victoria to the park eighteen miles away. The ruins have been cleared of brush, so the modern tourist probably can get a better view of Zimbabwe than Karl Mauch did when he climbed Zimbabwe hill in September of 1871.

By the time Mauch had returned to Europe and wrote up his experiences, he was convinced that he knew the origin of Zimbabwe. These ruins, Mauch said, are what remains of the fabulous Biblical land of Ophir, from which King Solomon had extracted so much gold. (Later the adventure writer H. Rider Haggard was to weave Zimbabwe into his most popular novel *King Solomon's Mines*, published in 1895. People knew the stories were fiction but millions accepted the existence of King Solomon's mines as sober fact.)

The Old Testament references to Ophir are brief and unenlightening:

"And king Solomon made a navy of ships in Ezion-geber, which is beside Eloth, on the shore of the Red Sea, in the land of Edom. And Hiram sent in the navy his servants, shipmen that had knowledge of the sea, with the servants of Solomon. And they came to Ophir, and fetched from thence gold, four hundred and twenty talents [another reference gives the figure as four hundred and fifty talents], and brought it to king Solomon."

This is all we know about Ophir. But since Solomon's gold hoards must have amounted to nearly twenty tons, Ophir was a land passionately hunted for centuries. Many spots from Peru to India have been identified as Ophir. In the sixteenth century the Portuguese picked up the Arab legend that linked the gold which came from the interior of southeast Africa with the gold of Ophir.

Mauch enlarged imaginatively on this simple identification. In the Acropolis of Zimbabwe, Mauch saw a copy of King Solomon's temple on Mount Moriah. The Elliptical Building could be nothing other than a copy of the palace in which the Queen of Sheba had stayed when she visited Solomon. He even credited the queen herself with the construction of the buildings, asserting she had imported Phoenician workmen to do the job.

The Zimbabwe-Ophir identification gained many adherents in scholarly circles, and was received enthusiastically by nineteenth-century Bible societies. Fundamentalists felt that materialist science, with its stress on evidence, had damaged the reputation of the literal truth of the Bible. Here, it seemed, was a chance to prove the historical accuracy of a number of Biblical statements.

Another group was also enthusiastic about the Zimbabwe-Ophir identification. These were the gold hunters. There is no doubt that a good deal of gold had been mined in Mashonaland throughout the centuries, for the land is dotted with ancient gold mines. By the turn of the century, thousands of gold claims had been staked out in Mashonaland, many of them around sites of ancient mining operations. The modern miners destroyed most of the archaeological evidence of ancient methods of gold mining and smelting.

The first man to try to find gold in the ruins of Great Zimbabwe itself was a South African trader named Willi Posselt who arrived in 1888. He found no gold, although he searched diligently. He did, however, find several slabs of soapstone, five feet long and a few inches thick, whose upper ends had been carved with the images of birds. He hacked the image from one of the slabs and carried it away, later selling it to the empire builder Cecil Rhodes.

Posselt noted that his native bearers held a reverent attitude toward the ruins, for they "sat down and solemnly saluted by clapping their hands."

Posselt's lack of success did not discourage others. In 1895 a prospector named Neal and two South African investors formed the elegantly titled Ancient Ruins Company, Limited, whose charter allowed it to "exploit all the ancient ruins south of the Zambesi." In five years Neal and his backers reported finding five hundred ounces of gold in forty-three different ruins. For prospectors this was a disappointing total, and for archaeologists it was a disaster. Although some of the gold was in raw ore, much of it came from jewelry and other objects that were simply melted down for their metallic value. Forty years later scientists were able to preserve a golden treasure found at Mapungubwe in the northern Transvaal. It gave a hint of what the "explorers of Ophir" must have destroyed.

Gold wasn't the only thing destroyed. If walls stood in the way, the gold hunters simply pushed them over. With their spades they hopelessly disrupted much stratigraphic evidence, so necessary to scientific archaeology.

The British Empire took possession of Mashonaland in 1891. Wrote one of the conquerers: "Today then, the Englishman is in the land of Ophir—opening afresh the treasure house of antiquity . . . we may expect to see the image of Queen Victoria stamped on the gold with which King Solomon overlaid his ivory throne, and wreathed the cedar pillars of his temple."

English control meant control by Cecil Rhodes—indeed the area was soon to be named Rhodesia in his honor. Rhodes viewed the depredations of the Ancient Ruins Company with disfavor. They were unprofitable and probably destroyed more than they found. Through Rhodes's influence, the company was forced to go out of business in 1900, and in 1902 the new government of Southern Rhodesia passed an ordinance for the protection of what was left of the ancient ruins.

Rhodes had been interested in the ruins of Zimbabwe for years. In 1901 he had sent the traveler and antiquary Theodore Bent there. Bent quickly succumbed to the Queen of Sheba–Phoenician–Ophir theory, and his extremely popular book, *Ruined Cities of Mashonaland*, helped spread the legend. In 1892 the archaeologist Sir John Willoughby went crashing through the ruins with the best of intentions and the worst of results.

Prospector Neal, late of the Ancient Ruins Company, Ltd., collaborated with a local journalist named Richard Hall and produced *Ancient Ruins of Rhodesia* in 1902. The Phoenicians and Sabaeans (Sheba's people) again got the credit. The book was so convincing that Hall came to be considered an expert, and in light of his great knowledge he was appointed curator of the Zimbabwe ruins. Enthusiastic and dedicated to his new job, Hall dug furiously for a couple of years. The result was the publication of *Great Zimbabwe* in 1905.

Mauch's original theory about the temple of Solomon had been refined. Hall saw Zimbabwe as having "a minimum age of three millenniums." It had been built in two stages. From 2000 to 1000 B.C. the construction was Sabaean; later, "somewhat anterior to 1100 B.C. down to some time before the Christian era," the construction was Phoenician.

The theory was attractive for several reasons. Both the Sabaeans (whose homeland was in Southern Arabia) and the Phoenicians (seafarers from the coast of Lebanon) were, and remain, rather mysterious peoples. Both had connections with Africa, the Phoenicians with Carthage, and the Sabaeans with Ethiopia. But most attractive of all to the theorizers was the knowledge that both peoples were white—well, not exactly white—swarthy, but certainly not black.

While the Phoenician-Sabaean theory remained most popular, Zimbabwe was also attributed to Arabs, Chinese, the Dravidians of India, Malays, and just about every other non-black people on earth. It was an article of faith in the early twentieth century that African Negroes were primitive savages who lived in mud huts and couldn't build anything. Besides, the idea that there had been white conquerors of Africa in antiquity gave historical justification to the current white conquerors who were busily slaughtering the natives.

Nor did the need for self-serving justification end when the wars ended. As late as 1950 white settlers were linking themselves with imaginary predecessors. Wrote one: "As they [the current settlers] build and mine and dream and die, can it be that history is using them to repeat itself? Did an ancient Motherland beyond the seas provide sons who, as aliens in Africa, mined and built and were overwhelmed? Is this the path we should follow beyond the vale of time?"

Zimbabwe today lies within Rhodesia, a country where a white minority is struggling to maintain supremacy over an overwhelming number of blacks. The ruins present white Rhodesians with a problem: they can't be ignored because they are a great tourist attraction. So the white Rhodesians try to ignore over half a century of careful archaeological investigation by playing up the "mystery" angle. Here is how the ruins are described in a brochure given out at Zimbabwe Ruins National Park:

"For the past 100 years, the Zimbabwe Ruins have been described as 'the great mystery' and 'the age-old riddle.' Ever since their discovery in 1868, they have intrigued not only archaeologists and other specialists, but also the many lay visitors attracted by the brooding atmosphere and the sense of some vanished civilization.

"Today, the scientific controversy still erupts from time to time, always deriving from conflicting opinions on who the builders of Zimbabwe were; and why they built the great edifice; but, whatever the true scientific explanation, the Ruins are certainly one of the greatest spectacles in Africa."

The trouble with this cautious statement is "the great mystery" of Zimbabwe was essentially solved in 1905 by a young British archaeologist, David Randall-MacIver, the first really qualified man to examine the ruins. What Randall-MacIver found was embarrassing to those of the mud-hut school of thinking about Africa. But he was quite clear: "the character of the dwellings contained within the stone ruins, and forming an integral part of them, is unmistakably African," and "the arts and manufactures exemplified by objects found within the dwellings are typically African . . ." In short, the builders of Zimbabwe, which the Europeans had been so quick to claim for Solomon and Sheba, were in reality the despised and persecuted Africans themselves.

Randall-MacIver had another bombshell, this one aimed at the romantics who adore speculating over vanished civilizations of incredible antiquity. After investigating Zimbabwe and seven other sites, he said he had not been able to find a single object "which can be shown to be more ancient than the fourteenth or fifteenth centuries." Zimbabwe just wasn't very old. The date for the first construction of Zimbabwe has been pushed back considerably since Randall-MacIver's time, but it is still nowhere near the time of Solomon.

Actually, the supporters of a non-African origin for Zimbabwe had really overestimated the technical difficulties involved in the construction, as well as underestimating the achievements of the Africans. Now they challenged their opponents to prove the existence of an unknown high order of black African civilization in the fourteenth or fifteenth centuries. Of course there was no such thing. Zimbabwe was built by a people who had reached a level of civilization roughly comparable to that of the Saxon invaders of the British Isles. It was a comparison that the descendants of the Saxons, who were greedily exploiting the descendants of of the Zimbabwe culture, were not going to accept easily. Moreover, these people were not unknown—they had regularly traded gold, much of which reached Europe. In return, the people of Zimbabwe received many European items— including Dutch gin.

Randall-MacIver was caustic concerning Richard Hall's methods and conclusions. Hall was not only unconvinced by Randall-MacIver, he was enraged by the charges that had been made against him. In 1909 he struck back with the volume *Prehistoric Rhodesia*, largely a replay of his previous theories. Randall-MacIver was equally contentious, and attacked again. A bitter and often highly personal feud raged between the two men for almost twenty years. People chose sides less on the basis of facts than on their attitudes toward Africans.

The controversy simply would not die, and it contained so many explosive political ramifications that a quarter century after the Randall-MacIver expedition the British Association (which had sponsored Randall-MacIver) felt it necessary to send out yet a second expedition. The leader of this expedition was Dr. Gertrude Caton-Thompson. Her report, *The Zimbabwe Culture*, brings up points of disagreement here and there with Randall-MacIver. For example, she sees possible Arab influences in the Conical Tower and the chevron design. But as to the builders of Zimbabwe there is no doubt: "Examination of all the existing evidence gathered from every quarter still can produce not one single item that is not in accordance with the claim of Bantu origin and medieval date." Elsewhere she states: "I am definitely unable to fall in with the oft-repeated and compromising suggestion that Zimbabwe and its allied structures were built by native workmen under the direction of a 'superior' alien race or supervisor."

This is not to imply that Miss Caton-Thompson had solved all the problems concerning Zimbabwe. She herself observed, "Zimbabwe is a mystery which lies in the still pulsating heart of native Africa." Nor have all the problems been solved today, despite repeated expeditions since Miss Caton-Thompson's in 1929. The latest major excavations at Zimbabwe were made in 1958, under the direction of Roger Summers, director of the National Museum of Southern Rhodesia. For the first time it became possible for a tentative outline of the history of Zimbabwe to be constructed. Not only did Summers use archaeological findings, but also Arab and Portuguese accounts of the black kingdoms of medieval Rhodesia, and the accounts of the modern inhabitants of the region about their own history. One African chief chided Summers, "If only you white people had asked the old people about Zimbabwe when you first came to the country, we'd all know a lot more about it now."

When Solomon was entertaining the Queen of Sheba, and sending ships to fetch the gold of Ophir, he could not possibly have sent them to Zimbabwe, because there was no Zimbabwe. The people who lived on the cliff later to be occupied by Zimbabwe were nomads with a stone age culture. Some crude paintings and their skeletons is all they left behind. The skeletons indicate these first inhabitants were of Bushmanoid rather than purely Negroid racial stock.

There are plenty of ancient gold mines in the Zimbabwe region, and archaeologists have been unable to determine the age of these mines, so it is possible—barely—that some of the gold of Ophir actually did come from that area, although it is much more likely that fabled Ophir was located far to the north on the Red Sea, in what is now Ethiopia. In any event, neither Solomon nor Sheba, nor the Phoenicians had anything to do with the stone buildings, because they were not constructed until centuries later.

Most likely, mining in the area began around A.D. 100, when a new people—distinctly Negroid this time and possessing a knowledge of the use of iron—moved into the area, probably attracted by gold. When the easy-to-reach gold was exhausted, these iron age folk started to dig for it. Shafts followed gold-bearing veins down a hundred feet or more. Space at the bottom of such shafts was so confined that only slender young girls could work in them. We know this because some were trapped in the shafts, and nearly two thousand years later archaeologists brought up the skeletons of the victims of these early mine disasters. Oddly, many of the skeletons in the shaft are those of girls of the Bushman type. Had the Bushman become miner slaves of the iron age Negroes, or had they learned the mining techniques for themselves? There is no answer, but it is clear the two peoples were living side by side.

By A.D. 400 the gold reachable by simple mining techniques was exhausted, or something else happened in the area, because Zimbabwe hill was abandoned for several hundred years.

About A.D. 1000 successive waves of cattle-raising people

began drifting into the Zimbabwe region. Numerous clay models of cows dating from the period indicate the chief concern of these people. One of these groups of migrants, says Summers, began building the stone walls of Great Zimbabwe around the eleventh or twelfth century.

In a general way we can name these first builders. They were the Shona people. Shona is a language and Shona-speaking people still live along the southeastern coast of Africa and still make the kind of pottery that is found in association with the earliest building at Zimbabwe.

When the Arab traders wandering through the interior first encountered the Shona of Zimbabwe, they were ruled by a king and priest who held the title Monomotapa. This information was eventually transmitted to the Portuguese, but the name became garbled, and Duarte Barbosa spoke of "the great kingdom of Benametapa." Portuguese sailors took the rumors of the kingdom to Europe, where to some it sounded as if the home of the legendary Prester John himself—the great Christian Priest-King who ruled a vast kingdom in some distant land—had finally been found.

Some seventeenth-century European geographers rather vaguely labeled all the unknown portions of inland Africa as part of the kingdom of the Monomotapa, the only ruler of whom they had heard. This is certainly an exaggeration, but his empire must have covered many thousands of square miles. The person of the Monomotapa was sacred, for he was a religious as well as a political figure, and his power was absolute within his own court. His empire, on the other hand, was probably not a tightly knit state. It is impossible to imagine that it could have been, owing to the incredible difficulty of communications over so vast and wild an area. The empire must have consisted of a group of powerful tribes, each ruling its own dominion but bound to the Monomotapa by ties of loyalty and religion much like those which bound vassals to their king and pope in early medieval Europe. Strong rulers could have exercised considerable power; during the reigns of weak ones, power must have tended to fragment.

At some dim time in history, the people who migrated to the land that was to become the empire of the Monomotapa brought with them metalworking skills from other civilizations. Some of the mining and smelting techniques may originally have come from Egypt, passed down through the Sudan to the Kingdom of Kush and then southward, from group to group, until they reached the group that came to the ore-rich lands around Zimbabwe. Other techniques of metal working may have come from the Arabs, who in the fourth century A.D. set up the kingdom of Axum in part of what is today Ethiopia. But the archaeology of the African interior is in its infancy. Any attempt to assign "cultural influences" over such a vast time and distance is pure guesswork, nothing more.

Although Zimbabwe is almost entirely a native African development, this does not mean that it was entirely isolated from the outside world. While Sir John Willoughby was burrowing recklessly through Zimbabwe's ruins in 1893 he found, under one of the earliest walls, what he called "pieces of sea-green china." Without a doubt, these were fragments of porcelain manufactured in twelfth- or thirteenth-century Sung Dynasty China. Inevitably the theory popped up that the Chinese had built Zimbabwe.

Years of propaganda about "darkest Africa" has left the impression that until Stanley and Livingstone the interior of Africa had been cut off from the outside world since the beginning of time. This is nonsense. During the days of the

Egyptian Empire, the pharaohs had sent their ships along the east coast of Africa to trade their goods for gold and spices from the interior. The trade was conducted with a rich land called Punt, which has never been exactly located. Naturally enough, some thought Zimbabwe was Punt, but there is better reason to believe that Punt was not quite so far south.

Greeks and Romans certainly traded with the people of the interior, and after them Arabs, Persians and Indians set up trading posts along the coast and carried on a regular and lively commerce with the people of the interior.

The people of the Zimbabwe culture seem to have valued gold mainly as an item of trade, but they did not export all of it. At least a small percentage was retained for its ornamental value. Barbosa mentioned the gold-bound scabbards of the men of Benametapa. Unfortunately, the gold hunters stripped Zimbabwe and its surrounding area of its gold. However, some two hundred miles to the south, just south of the Limpopo River, scientists got a chance to examine an undisturbed royal burial site.

The site was on a small steep "table mountain" of sandstone. There were few white men in the area in 1932, but all of them had heard rumors of a sacred hill. It was regarded as "a place of fear" by the Africans, who would not reveal its location. Finally, a farmer named van Graan found an African who gave away the secret and pointed out a hill called Mapungubwe. He also showed van Graan and three companions a hidden way up the steep hill.

On top the men found broken pots, iron implements and gold. A professional archaeologist, L. Fouche, describes what happened: "The party continued their search, scratching over the loose soil with their knives. They found large pieces of plate gold, some of them shaped. These were the remains of little rhinoceroses which had consisted of thin plate gold tacked by means of little gold tacks on to some core of wood or other substance which had perished. Solid gold tails and ears, beautifully made, had likewise been tacked on to these figures. Presently, they came upon the remains of a skeleton, which was dug out carefully; but the skull and most of the bones crumbled to dust on being exposed to the air."

Luckily, van Graan's son had studied archaeology with Fouche and convinced the others that it would be best to turn the site over to professionals rather than do the traditional thing and plunder it for the gold it contained.

What the van Graans had found was the first fully authenticated "royal burial ground" of pre-European times in southern Africa. Twenty-three skeletons were unearthed, one "wreathed in over a hundred bangles constructed of coiled wire. Several pieces of beautifully worked gold plating were also found, as well as about twelve thousand gold beads."

Many similar and probably greater burial grounds were destroyed by the gold-hungry plunderers of Zimbabwe.

Trade between the empire of the Monomotapa and the Arabs went on for a long time and they may have influenced some of the architectural features of Zimbabwe. Miss Caton-Thompson believes that the enigmatic Conical Tower was built in imitation of the minarets the Monomotapa's subjects had seen on the coast, and the chevron design on the walls may also have been influenced by similar designs used by the Arabs or other Islamic peoples.

In 1498 Vasco da Gama showed his Portuguese countrymen that it was possible to sail directly to Asia by going around the Cape of Good Hope. This not only opened up China and India to Portuguese traders, but the east coast of Africa as well. Da Gama himself planted the Portuguese colonies at Mozambique. But the Portuguese were not numerous or very adventurous when it came to inland exploring. They preferred to cling to their coastal trading posts and listen to the gossip of Arab merchants from the interior, and gaze wonderingly at the occasional band of skin-clad black men who had walked for twenty or thirty days to the coast in order to trade their gold for the products of other lands.

Ironically, when Barbosa was writing about "the great kingdom of Benametapa," the real kingdom of the Monomotapa had already passed its peak and was breaking up. Zimbabwe itself was still in control of the Monomotapa, but the former southern and eastern provinces of his empire were now ruled by a secessionist tribe called the Rozwi. The Portuguese were able to establish good relations with the Monomotapa and eventually to succeed in turning his empire into sort of a puppet state. But the Rozwi were made of sterner stuff, and resisted all Portuguese efforts. Hence the silence about Zimbabwe during the era of Rozwi ascendancy.

By the beginning of the eighteenth century the Rozwi were ruled by an extremely powerful and aggressive dynasty of kings whose title was Changamire or Mambo. They destroyed the creaky remnants of the Monomotapa's empire and took possession of Zimbabwe, which was to serve as a religious center for their empire. Rozwi Mambos held sway over an area which extended from the Zambezi River in the north to the mountains of Transvaal in the south, and from the Indian Ocean to that part of South Africa called Bechuanaland. It was an area of some 240,000 square miles, containing a million people, perhaps more. Trade was vigorous and the Rozwi left at Zimbabwe artifacts which had come from every part of the world, including some stone bottles from Holland which had once held Dutch gin.

The greatest irony is that while trade was going on between Zimbabwe and Europe, the Rozwi Mambos were busily rebuilding Zimbabwe. Their building techniques had improved considerably, and many of the ruins which so astounded Europeans and sent them scurrying about for ancient tales of Solomon and Sheba, were in reality little over a hundred years old.

Though it is impossible to reconstruct with any accuracy what life was like in the Zimbabwe of the Monomotapa, or of his successors, the Mambos, this has not stopped many people from trying. The German ethnologist, Leo Frobenius, saw sex as the basic reason behind the construction of Zimbabwe. "When this culture was at its height, the consummation of the king's nuptials must have been an extremely solemn affair. It could not take place in any room, but had to be performed upon a platform which in the early stages must have been erected on a kind of tower. Such unions served a religious function and were timed according to the positions of the stars."

Frobenius also liked to locate Atlantis in Africa. He published his speculations in the early 1930s at about the same time Miss Gertrude Caton-Thompson's book on Zimbabwe was published. The careful archaeology of Miss Caton-Thompson was almost completely eclipsed in public favor by Frobenius' juicy speculations.

Nor is Frobenius forgotten today. George and Herman Schreiber, popular writers on archaeological and historical subjects, pick up his story of the king's mating and continue: "The purpose of the granite monoliths on the Acropolis at Zimbabwe, which have generally been viewed as phallic symbols, now become clear. Here, close to the sky, the king who still symbolized the god slept with the earth-mother goddess who symbolized the god's sister, the evening star." Doubtful, to say the least.

There is, however, little doubt that Zimbabwe had great religious significance. Even today shrines where the natives of the area carry on their religious rites may be referred to as "the real Zimbabwe." For the Mambos, Zimbabwe was purely a religious center. Their political capital was Manyanga, a hundred miles north.

The most frequently repeated story of life under the Monomotapa was that he was always accompanied by a body-guard. When the guard got bored they sent up a cry "nyam, nyam," which means "meat, meat." To appease them, the Monomotapa would pick out some unlucky bystander, who would immediately be killed and devoured. The practice led to the perfectly understandable superstition that it was un-lucky to look the Monomotapa in the face.

This was the sort of exotic story Europeans have delighted in reporting. It may be an accurate account, an exaggeration, or a complete falsehood. There is no way of telling.

While the beginnings of Zimbabwe are still misty, the de-tails of its fall are well known.

The end of the empire of the Rozwi Mambos, and of Zimbabwe itself, was swift and complete. At the beginning of the nineteenth century the once obscure tribe of the Zulus had begun to coalesce into a mighty nation. Under the brilliant and terrifying leadership of their chief, Shaka, the Zulu warriors drove all their enemies before them. The Nguni, a tribe closely related to the Zulus, were no match for Shaka's troops and fled northward, reaching the southern borders of the Mambos' empire about 1830.

The Nguni themselves were fierce and barbaric people, and although the Rozwi had perhaps once been the finest fighters in Africa, years of comfortable rule had softened them. The Nguni swept through the Rozwi Empire like a plague of locusts. By 1833 they had sacked Zimbabwe and slaughtered its inhabitants. A year later they trapped the last Mambo, Chirisamuru, at Manyanga and had him flayed alive. By 1835 the Rozwi Empire simply ceased to exist and the Nguni, finding nothing left to pillage, moved on.

A few survivors crept back to the ruins of Zimbabwe. They built some crude dwellings and tried to carry on the old ceremonies, but the priests had been slaughtered, and knowledge of the rites had died with them. Finally, only a few of the Rozwi, perhaps only one, an old man called Babareke, remained at Zimbabwe. A mere thirty-seven years after the destruction of Zimbabwe Karl Mauch, his clothes in tatters, but his romantic imagination still intact, came walking into the "place of stones."

Babareke tried to tell Mauch what had happened, and tried to relate what he could recall of the old rites, but Mauch understood nothing. He thought Babareke was describing ancient Semitic rites, and the legend-building began.

Today, very few hold out for the white origin of Zimbabwe. Only among the white minority in Rhodesia, where the concept of black inferiority is necessary for the maintenance of their state, is there any real argument about who built Zimbabwe.

The name of Zimbabwe has not yet passed into ancient history. As African states have become independent, they have reached back into their own histories to find traditional names to replace those appended by white colonists. Rhodesia is still under white control, but, given the tide of events in Africa, it is unlikely to remain so forever. Black nationalists of Rhodesia have already chosen a name for their new nation—it will be called Zimbabwe.

THE OLMEC HEARTLAND

Bearded Men and Baby Faces

A satisfaction of archaeology in the Middle East is that you can get a pretty clear picture of how and where it all began. In Jericho, the oldest continuously inhabited city in the world, archaeologists have dug down through layer after layer of debris left by previous inhabitants, right down to sterile soil. From this they have been able to reconstruct the development of life in that city. The origins of the Sumerians, the earliest known civilization, remain unclear, but excavations in Mesopotamia have revealed that all other civilizations in the region developed from their model.

The same satisfying state has not yet been reached regarding the great civilizations of Mexico and South America. They are like a Chinese box puzzle. Every time the origins of one are found, right behind it is another great civilization equally well developed. Where and how did it all begin? Who were the Sumerians of the Americas? This question has spawned the most extravagant possible fantasies. Within the last few years a series of astonishing discoveries in Veracruz and Tabasco in Mexico may finally give us the answer. But what an answer! It poses more puzzles than it could possibly solve.

It is all too new, too strange. The way-out theorists, the occultists and lovers of the bizarre have not yet had time to wrap their imaginations around this new enigma. Let us take a look at the area along the Gulf Coast of Mexico which was the heartland of a people we call the Olmecs.

When Hernán Cortés entered Mexico he encountered the Aztecs, whose civilization in many respects equaled or surpassed that of his native Spain. Although the Aztecs tried to glorify their own past it was clear they were newcomers, relative barbarians, who had taken much from the people they conquered. Indeed the Aztecs had ruled the Valley of Mexico for only two generations before their power was broken by the European invaders.

At the time of Cortés, Europeans had not yet heard of the Mayan Indians. The Spanish had encountered Mayans but were not impressed, because by the time the Spanish arrived the highpoint of Maya civilization had long since passed. What remained was a pale reflection of their time of greatness.

Maya civilization was not really discovered until the late 1830s, when a young American traveler, John Lloyd Stephens, accompanied by artist Frederick Catherwood, toured the jungles that had smothered the former Maya domain uncovering cities and monuments of unbelievable strangeness and magnificence. There had been hints before, but it was Stephens' careful observations and gracefully written account, aided immeasurably by Catherwood's superb drawings, that brought the Maya to the attention of the world.

The effect was electrifying. Although Stephens was moderate, and usually correct in his theories, everyone else seemed to go quite mad. The Maya were suddenly catapulted from obscurity to the position of being the Greeks of ancient America, the purest survivors of the lost continent of Atlantis, the Ten Lost Tribes, the first civilized people in the world and so on. The impression persists that there is something immeasurably ancient and immeasurably great about the Maya.

In an enormous, gorgeously illustrated tome by Robert B. Stacy-Judd published in 1939 we find this dedication:

"To that great race of people who, among other outstanding accomplishments, created from the natural plant life numerous items now comprising our staple diet, who excelled as astronomers, founded a calendar without equal, gave us the zero symbol, originated an unique system of writing, established a classic architectural style, erected cities of beauty and permanence, believed in One God and the Immortality of the Soul, possessed no ships of war, maintained no army of aggression, required no prisons, suffered little from disease, and who, until assailed, lived for centuries in peace and happiness—THE ANCIENT MAYAS."

The name of Stacy-Judd's book is *Atlantis: Mother of Empires*. Naturally the author believes the Maya came from the lost continent.

The Maya were without doubt an extraordinary people. But their accomplishments, most particularly their peaceful nature, have been exaggerated beyond all reason. They were probably not as bloodthirsty as the Aztecs who had just risen from barbarism, but they were every bit as warlike as most other Central American civilizations, which means they were pretty bloodthirsty indeed. Among their other accomplishments, it must be added that they may well have been the first people to shrink heads successfully.

Before the Maya there were the Toltecs, who for a long

time remained a semi-legendary people. Everything that was unexplained about the Maya was ascribed to the Toltecs. They were even credited with constructing the great burial mounds of the central portions of North America. So great became their reputation that scholars began to wonder if Toltec was not simply a word which meant "master builder." Ultimately, however, a genuine Toltec culture was found, but this did not solve any problems because the Toltecs too turned out to be latecomers.

In his collection of the writings of archaeologists in the Americas, *Conquistadors Without Swords,* Dr. Leo Deuel observes, "Antecedents had their antecedents. Thus the builders of Teotihaucán in the Valley of Mexico and of Tajín on the Gulf Coast, and the Mixtecs and Zapotecs in southern Mexico came into their own. Each in turn, for a brief moment in scholarship, might enjoy the reputation of having evolved the arts of civilization all on their own in this part of the globe, only to have their exalted position just as quickly challenged."

With such a history, it would be presumptuous and foolish to claim that the Olmecs are the starting point on the road to civilization in the Americas. But right now they are the most promising candidates. In any event, the Olmecs represent something extremely significant, and unique, in pre-Columbian civilization.

The Olmecs were really imagined before they were ever discovered. They were born in the educated speculations of George Clapp Vaillant, well before there was any real evidence that anything that might be called an Olmec culture existed. Vaillant was a pioneer of Mexican archaeology. He also had a "flair" for recognizing and differentiating art styles.

Vaillant's inspiration for the Olmecs was a single artifact— a little jade tiger or ocelot which reposed in the Mexican hall of the American Museum of Natural History. "Plastically," wrote Vaillant, "the tiger belongs to a group of sculptures which all exhibit the same features, a snarling tiger mouth surmounted by a flat pugnose and oblique eyes." Vaillant found this "tiger face" class "tends to merge with a group of carvings which, although having infantile features, retain the contorted mouth of tiger sculptures." These sculptures which Vaillant labeled "baby face" seemed to come from the same general geographical area as the "tiger face" pieces.

From there Vaillant went on to consideration of a racial group, "characterized by flat noses, oblique eyes, low fore-heads, and often beards." He found a number of pieces of art depicting individuals of this type, and they all could be traced back to the same area which brought forth the "tiger face" and "baby face" sculptures.

Here Vaillant made a speculative leap: "When a physical type can be linked to an art style there is strong likelihood that we are dealing with the makers of that style. It sometimes happens that people take as national symbols those animals most resembling them in appearance or psychology . . ."

The flat-nosed bearded men did not merely appear on oc-casional pieces of art of unknown origin. Vaillant had found at least two examples showing these people in contact with other known peoples. "One of these is the painting on the celebrated Chama vase where a number of Mayas are shown receiving a flat-nosed bearded ambassador. The other is one of the murals at the Temple of the Warriors at Chichén Itzá, where the Mexican inhabitants of Chichén are shown giving a resounding beating to a group of flat-nosed tribesmen, some of whom have whiskers."

Dr. Deuel describes most of the flat-nosed bearded people as having a "bulgy-eyed, chubby look remindful of Greek satyrs." But not all bearded figures had flat noses. Another group possessed, along with their whiskers, narrow, beaked noses. With flowing beards and profuse mustaches, these beak-nosed figures looked distinctly non-Indian. A member of an archaeological expedition first encountering such a figure said it was the spitting image of Mephistopheles in a slick operatic production.

It was widely noted that many of the Mexican gods, most particularly the great god Quetzalcoatl, were often depicted as bearded. The idea of bearded gods even seems to have filtered as far down as the Inca civilization of Peru. Virtually every history of the Spanish conquest contains the observation that both Francisco Pizarro's defeat of the Incas and Cortés' defeat of the Aztecs were eased because the Indians of both nations believed that the white-skinned bearded Spaniards were somehow representative of the great god Quetzalcoatl, who had also been white-skinned and bearded. Certainly the Indians were struck and disconcerted by the appearance of the Spaniards, but how godlike they seemed we do not know. Their steel armor, firearms and horses, all of which were totally unfamiliar to the Indians, may have been as striking as their pale skins and beards. One even wonders just how "white" the Spaniards looked. Most of them must have been swarthy to begin with, and long exposure to the sun should have darkened their complexions to a shade not much lighter than that of the Indians themselves. Even the idea that Quetzalcoatl was white or had a lighter skin than the rest of the people is questionable—but there is no doubt that he and other gods were often depicted with beards.

The whole rediscovery of the high civilizations of Central and South America created a great deal of excitement in Europe and North America among people who were white,

European in background and possessors of a Judeo-Christian heritage. They were accustomed to regarding themselves as superior, but they were now confronted with the possibility that people who were not white, not European and who had never had the advantage of the Old and New Testament, were able to create a civilization. Many could not accept this. The reasons behind their disbelief ranged from simple racism to a philosophical conviction that civilization could start only in one place and could not develop independently in several different places at different times.

The overwhelming belief was that Indian civilization had not started among the Indians. In this hypothesis, the bearded figures assume major importance. The Indians of Central and South America are of Mongolian stock. In general, today they either have very scanty beards or are entirely beardless. Who, then, provided the inspiration for these bearded figures?

The theorists concentrated on the bearded figures with the high straight noses and ignored the numerous flat-nosed bearded figures. When they did discuss the second type they mentioned only the beards, and failed to note that in other respects these figures looked distinctly non-white.

To some the high-nosed bearded figures looked Semitic. Many believed that the wandering Ten Lost Tribes of Israel had had their day in America. This theory was so influential that an Englishman visiting Indian villages said that he felt just as if he were back in the Jewish quarter of London.

Christians refused to be bested. To them the bearded figures were clearly a group of wandering Irish monks. To anthropologist Thor Heyerdahl they were his own Viking ancestors. To others they were Phoenicians or Romans or what have you. What tied all these theories together was the idea that it was these advanced light-skinned people, not the Indians, who had begun civilization in the Americas.

The beard evidence proves nothing and is a point open to a multitude of interpretations. For example, it would be perfectly possible for a black nationalist to claim, on the strength of the bearded figures, that it was black Africans who brought civilization to the Western Hemisphere. The flat-nosed bearded figures look far more like Negroes than they do Europeans or Semites. How about the high-nosed bearded figures? Look at Emperor Haile Selassie of Ethiopia—he is a black African with a high thin nose and a full beard.

There are also figures found throughout the Americas that look more Chinese than Indian, and indeed some have claimed that Indian civilization was brought by migrants from China. The question of trans-Atlantic and trans-Pacific contacts is far from settled. It is quite possible, probable even, that such contacts did take place. But even if they did there is no evidence that they were anything more than occasional, and they had no lasting significance. All the major elements of the great civilizations of the Western Hemisphere seem to have developed in the Western Hemisphere.

The bearded men were none other than native South Americans themselves. We tend to think of the Indians as a single pure racial type. But this is not true; in pre-Columbian times there were many different physical types. No country is racially pure. In Japan, for example, there is a hirsute group called the Ainus who live among the smooth-skinned, Mongolian-type Japanese. The Ainu may have been in Japan longer than the Japanese themselves. Such a group also may have existed in the Americas. In any case there were plenty of bearded Indians when the Spanish arrived. Leo Deuel says, "Spaniards landing in Panama noted that the natives sported finer beards than they had themselves. Pure-breed bearded Indians were met by explorers among the Taironas in northern Colombia. Nordenskjöld described them in the southern Andes of Bolivia." Dr. Deuel concludes that all the stories about pre-Columbian landings of white men or tales of a superior group of light-skinned bearded rulers and conquerors are nothing more than "worn-out twaddle."

In 1932 George C. Vaillant did not have to go to Europe or the Middle East to find the origins of the bearded folk. He linked the bearded figures, the "tiger faces" and the "baby faces" together and said they might all in some way represent an ancient Mexican people, the Olmecs.

It was a bold guess. Olmec was nothing more than a name in some ancient legends. But Vaillant believed in ancient legends. "Now, it sometimes happens that bygone peoples are transmuted by folk-lore into mythological beings . . . In Mexico we find the Toltecs, who preceded the Aztecs in the Valley of Mexico, endowed by their successors with almost supernatural skills in the arts. Perhaps in the same way the bearded people were thus considered, and certain of their chieftains or even mayhap their gods were absorbed . . ."

Vaillant went through the legends eliminating one people after another, until finally, ". . . there is often described in the traditions a highly civilized people called the Olmec . . . They were famed for their work in jade and turquoise, and were credited with being the chief users of rubber in Central America." Olmec means "rubber people."

The geographical distribution mentioned in the legends for the Olmecs roughly coincided with the area from which the "tiger face" and "baby face" sculptures were believed to come.

It was sheer speculation because as Vaillant himself said:

"No formal excavation has been undertaken in the Olmec area and we know nothing of their beginnings nor of their relations to other cultures. The Olmecs move like shadows across the pages of Mexican history; a few notices that there were such people, a few delineations of a physical type foreign to the racial features of the known peoples like the Maya, and a handful of sculptures out of the known artistic traditions comprise the testimony of their existence. Perhaps investigation in the Olmec area would clarify the much discussed relationship between the Mexicans and the Mayas, or even reveal the origin of the great theocracies that gave Central America its civilization."

In some ways the map of Mexico resembles the rear end of a fish. The body curves and narrows before fanning out into a tail, which is Yucatán. The Olmec area lies in the narrow curved portion of the body, along the Gulf of Mexico side. It is part of the modern states of Veracruz and Tabasco. The land is low, for the most part swampy steamy jungle. It has no obvious ruins comparable to those found in the Valley of Mexico or Yucatán, yet Vaillant pointed this area out as the possible starting place of all Mesoamerican civilizations.

In addition to the small sculptures that had actually been found in these coastal lowlands, there were stories that several colossal sculptures unlike anything ever seen before had been encountered in the jungle. In the 1860s a Mexican engineer reported seeing an enormous stone head with "Ethiopian" features.

In 1938, six years after Vaillant published his daring speculations about the Olmecs, American archaeologist Matthew W. Stirling of the Smithsonian Institution began excavations in the Gulf area. Within months Vaillant's thesis was brilliantly and spectacularly confirmed.

Stirling's first major find, made at a place called Tres Zapotes, was one of those enormous "Ethiopian" heads. The head, and it was ony a disembodied head, lacking even a neck, was made of basaltic rock, and was over seven feet tall. It weighed upwards of twenty tons. Later Stirling located four more of these heads at La Venta, an island of high ground in the midst of a dense mangrove swamp, and obviously an important Olmec site. These Olmec "heads" have become the most famous of all Olmec sculptures. Each has its own individual characteristics, but all follow the same basic pattern. They all show chubby round-faced young men. The thick lips and broad noses give the heads a Negroid look—hence the early description of them as Ethiopian. But the eyes are slanted and Mongoloid. Some of the mouths are curved into a subtle smile, displaying a set of nicely rounded teeth. Others are masked with an expression of awesome serenity. All wear earplugs, sideburns and what looks like a football helmet. Aside from the earplugs these statues could be portraits of tough beefy linemen from a professional football team.

There is no doubt that these colossal heads are unique, artistic masterpieces which compare favorably with the best art produced by the ancient civilizations of Europe and the Middle East. Miguel Covarrubias, a popular Mexican artist turned archaeologist, said of the heads and other pieces of colossal sculpture dug up by Stirling that they "are among the largest, most thrilling examples of early Indian art. The carving on the monoliths is sensitive and realistic, with a unique mastery of technique and creative expression. The sculptures are free of many of the vices that contaminate much of the later Indian art: stilted stylization, stifling overloading of ritualistic detail, and a purely decorative flamboyancy."

Next to the heads, the most compelling discoveries made by Stirling were of statues and other representations of what Vaillant had called the "baby face" type.

Covarrubias' description of this type of figure is the best available. He says they are representations of "squat, fat men with elongated pear-shaped heads, small perforated noses, fat necks, heavy jowls and stubborn chins. Their eyes are decidedly Mongoloid—almond-shaped or narrow slits between puffed eyelids. But their most characteristic feature is a large despondent mouth, with the corners drawn downwards and a thick, flaring upper lip, like a snarling jaguar's. It is evident that these artists meant to represent a definite, traditional concept—a plump character with short but well-made arms and legs and with small hands and feet, either standing or seated crosslegged, Oriental fashion. They are generally shown nude and sexless, or wearing a simple loincloth or a short skirt with an ornamental buckle in front. There is always a strong feline feeling, coupled with a haunting infantile character and expression about their faces, as if they were meant to represent a totemic prototype, half-jaguar, half-baby, so characteristic and powerful that it is short of being an obsession. In fact, many of these sculptures are actually jaguars or rather a jaguar deity, perhaps a jaguar cub-ancestor, since so often their snarling mouths show toothless gums." Later, scholars were to call these figures "children of the jaguar" or "were-jaguars."

Bearded figures also turned up in Stirling's excavations. The most striking was carved on a stone slab or stela. It shows two elaborately dressed men facing one another. The face of the man on the left has been deliberately smashed beyond recognition. But the man on the right possesses an enormous aquiline nose, totally different from the typical flat-nosed people.

Covarrubias says the figure has "surprisingly pronounced Semitic features."

Stirling could only guess at the age of these Olmec monuments, because radiocarbon dating was not available in the 1930s (stone monuments cannot be dated radioactively, but charcoal and other objects found in association with them can). But every indication was that they were far older than Maya, Toltec or any other artifacts. They seemed in fact the oldest monuments in Mexico.

Back in 1902 a small Olmec-type figure of a fat bald man wearing a duck disguise was found near the Olmec site of Tres Zapotes. Sculpted into the stomach of this jadite figure was a glyph of an undecipherable type. Along with the glyph, however, was a date. This the archaeologists could read because it corresponded to the Mayan dating system, which had already been deciphered. If the date was correct the statue was made in, or at least dated, 98 B.C., long before the rise of the Maya. Besides, Maya culture was not known to have penetrated as far as Tres Zapotes.

Then at Monte Alban, stronghold of the Zapotic culture, the oldest relief sculptures were of a distinctly non-Zapotic type. These grotesque rhythmic figures looked Olmec. The Olmecs, it seemed, were ancestral to both Mayas and Zapotics.

Baby faces, beards, jaguars and colossal "football players"— these were the enigmatic traces of the Olmecs. A tremendous amount of discussion swept Mexican archaeological circles, but none of it seemed to get anyone nearer to a solution of what came to be called the Olmec Puzzle. Stirling, although his finds were magnificent, had barely scratched the surface of the sites in the Olmec heartland. The United States was engaged in the Second World War and money and archaeological personnel became unavailable, and Mexico simply did not have the resources to conduct extensive excavations. Interest in the Olmecs picked up in the mid-1950s when radiocarbon dating came up with some startlingly early dates for Olmec sites. However, it was not until the 1960s that archaeologists again made a concerted attack on the mysteries of the Olmec heartland.

The leading figure of this new generation of Olmec archaeologists is Dr. Michael Coe of the Department of Anthropology of Yale University. Coe's success at finding buried Olmec monuments has been remarkable. He looks over the ground of a likely Olmec site, points to a particular spot and orders his workmen to dig. Often, just three or four feet under the surface, they uncover an Olmec statue. According to Coe his workmen say he has "eyes that can see through the ground."

But there is nothing supernatural about Dr. Coe's abilities. He has discovered at least one of the secrets of the Olmec heartland. The monuments did not sink into the earth through the haphazard actions of time. They were carefully and systematically buried, centuries ago. Dr. Coe believes he is able partially to recognize the burial pattern and therefore anticipate where statues are buried. He estimates that there are thousands of buried statues at San Lorenzo, one Olmec site which he has excavated. And there are other, perhaps larger Olmec sites in the heartland. The area dubbed the heartland stretches along the coast for some 250 miles and penetrates inland up to eighty miles.

Dr. Coe has found out something else about the buried statues—all of them, including the gigantic heads of which twenty have now been uncovered, have been broken or mutilated in some way.

The amount of labor involved in this task of destruction

must have been enormous. Dr. Coe believes the colossal heads were marred with a two-pronged instrument, because each one of them bears two deep, unexplainable pockmarks. The surface may also have been defaced, but we can't be sure, for all that remains now is the rough basalt. Only one head retains a portion of its original smooth, skinlike finish. This head also retains a trace of paint, indicating that the heads were once completely colored.

Smaller monuments may have been hoisted up and dropped, or bashed with stone hammers. After the destruction, the monuments were dragged to a special place and laid in a pit floored with red gravel. Basketloads of earth, broken pottery and rocks were dumped over them. The larger monuments are still marked by small mounds. There are so many mounds in the San Lorenzo area that until Dr. Coe discovered their origins everyone believed them to be natural features of the landscape. Thousands of Olmec artifacts may lie buried beneath them.

If the destruction was complete, there is also something reverent and ritualistic about it. The common explanation for the fall of Olmec civilization is that they succumbed to some sort of invasion. But would outsiders destroy a city in such a manner? Dr. Coe thinks not. He is confident that the destruction was the result of some sort of internal convulsion, perhaps a revolution. Although the victors of this revolution overthrew the old rulers, they still retained the old traditions and religion. This meant that the monuments, which must have had sacred significance, had to be buried according to ritual.

But if the Olmecs took great pains in destroying their monuments they must also have taken great pains in building them. La Venta, San Lorenzo and other Olmec centers are deep in the swampy jungles. The nearest source of basalt, from which many of the great monuments have been fashioned, is the slopes of the Cerro Cintepec in the Tuxtla Mountains. These mountains are up to one hundred miles away from some of the Olmec sites. The blocks from which the monuments were sculpted must have been floated down rivers to the Gulf of Mexico on rafts, then along the coast, and finally dragged overland to the Olmec city.

In the hot, moist climate of the Olmec heartland only stone endures. Stirling excavated a tomb, but the body it had once contained had completely disintegrated over the years. What other materials might the Olmecs have used? It's possible they were superlative woodcarvers, or weavers, but neither wood nor cloth will long survive in such a climate. How about books? The Olmecs had a written language, and the Maya, whose language was apparently close to that of the Olmecs, did produce books, a few of which survive until the present day. An Olmec literature may have been entirely lost.

There was some discussion as to whether the Olmec sites actually were cities or merely ritual centers, used only for ceremonial occasions, and that the people lived in surrounding villages. Dwelling places were probably of wood and straw and have perished without a trace. Some artificial mounds which survive may once have been used to raise houses above the sodden soil, but this is speculation. Dr. Coe's excavations, however, strongly indicate that San Lorenzo, at least, was a population as well as a civil and religious center. Diggers uncovered a few hundred yards of what must have been an enormous and complex system of waterworks for both drainage and irrigation. Rain is abundant, sometimes up to 120 inches a year in the Olmec heartland, but it falls only in the rainy season. During dry periods water is scarce. The Olmecs collected water in tightly covered basalt troughs and piped it into artificial ponds or lagoons. The network of troughs was so well built that it still functions, although it has been untended for over two thousand years.

Before the development of radiocarbon dating, the earliest date that could be placed on Olmec civilization was 98 B.C. But radiocarbon dating of samples from San Lorenzo, accompanied by other dating methods, have pushed this early date back considerably. According to Dr. Coe the Olmec monuments at that site cannot have been constructed later than 900 or 800 B.C., and perhaps considerably earlier.

"We have, therefore, found the oldest civilized communities thus far known in Mesoamerica. Nonetheless, by pushing back the earliest Olmec civilization to such an early date—to a time when there was little else but simple village cultures in the rest of Mexico and Central America—the lack of antecedents is an embarrassing problem. We now have no idea where the Olmec came from or who built the mounds and carved the sculptures of San Lorenzo. Whoever they were, these pioneers must have been unusually gifted in engineering as well as art . . ."

The San Lorenzo area, in Dr. Coe's opinion, was the earliest site of Olmec civilization. Somewhere about 800 B.C. it was abandoned. Many of the monuments were ceremonially buried, and others presumably were dragged to a new Olmec center at La Venta. La Venta was in turn abandoned or destroyed after 400 B.C. After that, only flickerings of Olmec culture can be found at other sites.

The legends of the Aztecs concerning the Olmecs are extremely vague and confusing. Indeed, no one is quite sure whether the Olmecs referred to by the Aztecs were the same people who carved the jaguar-baby sculptures or not. Some scholars find the term Olmec so misleading that they have tried to have the term "La Venta" adopted for the mysterious culture. But Olmec has stuck, and unless we find out what these people called themselves, it is as good as any label.

Aztec legends also speak of a golden age which existed long ago in an apparently legendary land called "Tamoanchan." In some unclear way "Tamoanchan" was the land in which everything began. It is just one of many Aztec legends, but the land of "Tamoanchan" attracted the attention of scholars dealing with the "Olmec puzzle" because "Tamoanchan" is not an Aztec word; rather, it seems to come directly from archaic Maya. Many believe that there was some overlap between Olmec civilization and that civilization attributed to the Maya. There are two translations of "Tamoanchan." One is the "Land of Rain and Mist," a fitting description for the steamy jungle lowlands of the Olmec heartland. The second meaning is "Bird-Serpent," a symbol that recurs in Olmec art and in all later Mesoamerican art. The feathered serpent is the symbol of Quetzalcoatl, the "bearded" god.

Dr. Coe speculated that the Olmecs actually were the earliest Maya, but that the Mayas' memories of their own origins were contained only in legend. These in turn were picked up by the later Aztecs, who transmitted them in an even more blurred fashion to the Spanish, and finally to the modern scholars who are trying hard to untangle the puzzle. Covarrubias once commented that the Olmec riddle had "grown so complex that it is just short of incomprehensible even to most archaeologists, who handle it with the repugnance with which they handle a rattlesnake."

The lack of any Olmec skeletons places the problem of who the Olmecs were beyond our reach. Were they the flat-nosed bearded people, so often depicted? If they were, who then were the big-nosed bearded strangers? And if the Olmecs were early Mayas, why were the classic Mayas traditionally beardless, with enormous noses?

We can, however, make a few guesses as to the significance of the haunting jaguar-baby motif. On close examination the figures have a look suggesting Mongoloidism or cretinism. Dr. Coe believes that such children were worshiped by the Olmecs. These children with their strange appearance and actions may have reinforced the Olmec belief that there could be gods that were part jaguar and part human.

Many of the jaguar-baby figures also have a cleft in their foreheads. There are some birth deformities in which the soft spot in a baby's skull never closes properly. Many ancient societies regarded birth defects as signs from the gods, or saw deformed people as somehow being specially marked or favored by the gods. The Olmecs seem to have shared this belief.

A final guess concerns the great stone heads. They are usually described as portraits of Olmec war lords, but it is just possible they are exactly what they look like—football players, or at least ballplayers of some sort. Throughout ancient Mesoamerica, the Indians of many cultures were addicted to a game that resembled basketball. Ball courts are a central feature of most Indian cities. The object of the game was to get a hard rubber ball through a stone hoop, without the player using his hands. The hoop was high and small, so scores were not frequent, but what made the game exciting were the stakes. Winners might collect a fortune, losers might lose their lives as well as the game. Naturally, games were hard-fought and followed with great interest by the spectators.

Players wore a particular uniform, including a helmet like

those on the great stone heads. Therefore, rather than war lords, these smooth-faced young men might be athlete heroes. A great problem in thinking about a culture like the Olmecs is that we know so little that we tend to impose stereotypes of what an ancient culture *should* be like. An unknown building almost always is referred to as a temple just because we don't know what else to call it and all primitive peoples should have temples. For the same reason an unknown portrait is a war lord rather than an athlete, because we think war is serious business and sports are frivolous. But the Greeks and the Romans both erected numerous statues to their favorite athletes, and what about our own baseball hall of fame?

This appealing identification may be wrong, it may even be silly, but it helps to relieve some of the strangeness and grimness of our view of the Olmecs with their recurrent theme of deformed babies. When viewing one of their colossal statues we should think, "Perhaps this is old number thirty-two, who on one memorable afternoon in September scored two fantastic goals against the visitors from San Lorenzo and clinched the all-Olmec championship for the home team."

TEN

W

EL DORADO

~

Home of the Gilded Phantom

There might be something grand or funny about the search for El Dorado. After all, there were all those grown men hacking their way back and forth through the jungles of South America, often retracing one another's footsteps. Nothing, not even the fact that many others had already been there before them, could convince these seekers that they were not heading directly for the city of *el hombre dorado*, the gilded man.

It *might* be grand or funny, but one is continually being brought up short by the absolute horror of the search. There is a tinge of madness about everyone and everything connected with the story of El Dorado.

At first it made some sense. Men have always searched for golden cities and at the beginning of the sixteenth century two men had found them. Following vague rumors, Hernán Cortés located and conquered the kingdom of the Aztecs in 1521. When the gold of the Aztecs reached Spain, people saw what fabulous fortunes could be gained. There was a stampede to join expeditions going to the New World. So many went that a contemporary Spaniard observed that Spain "was left almost to the women."

Then it happened again! Rumors of an even wealthier kingdom, far to the south of the Aztec realm, had reached Spanish ears. In 1532 Francisco Pizarro and a handful of men conquered the Inca realm, and into the hands of the Spanish flowed a treasure that eclipsed even that which Cortés had plundered in Mexico.

Charles V, King of Spain, and through a series of dynastic accidents also ruler of half of the rest of Europe, was delighted. Keeping his rickety realm together was expensive and he needed all the gold he could get. The common people too were delighted. Poor men saw members of Pizarro's army—ordinary soldiers who had once been poor like themselves—suddenly become wealthy as dukes.

Spain was a poor and harsh country which had just finished a long series of exhausting wars with the Moors. The news of Pizarro's Peruvian conquests, coming on top of what Cortés had already found in Mexico, seemed like a miracle, a mark of God's special favor for the nation.

Could there be more golden realms in the Americas? Why not! As far as the Spanish were concerned they owned the New World. But they had only a vague notion of its size. At first they stuck to the coasts. But Cortés and Pizarro had found their cities of gold by striking inland.

The Spanish conquistadors were an extraordinary mixture of inexhaustable greed, inhuman cruelty, and rampaging religious fanaticism. The pursuit of gold had somehow become mystically linked with the spread of Christianity, and murder and torture became not so much a pleasure as an economic and religious necessity. The Spanish, however, dislike the judgments of historians of other nations on the actions of the conquistadors. Attempts to counter what they consider the "black legend" of Spanish atrocities have not been very successful. About all that can be said is that the conquistadors were extremely brave, and some of them were no worse than anyone else would have been in similar circumstances.

The history of El Dorado gives this argument some weight because the first men to begin the terrifying and blood-drenched search for the golden man were Germans.

German involvement in South America came about as a result of the complicated financial dealings of Charles V. In order to add yet another crown to his collection, Charles wished to be elected Holy Roman Emperor. The title carried little real power, but it had been in his family for centuries. Theoretically the Holy Roman Emperor was chosen by the votes of seven European princes called electors. When Charles' grandfather died, the office of Holy Roman Emperor fell vacant, and Francis I, King of France, and Henry VIII of England decided to contend for it. The only sure way of being elected was to bribe the electors. Henry quickly dropped out of the running, but Francis ruled a rich country, and the stakes rose. Charles emptied his coffers and began looking around for money to borrow. One of his sources was the newly powerful German banking family, the Welsers. They loaned him 143,000 gold florins. Charles won the office but was unable to pay his debts. So to mollify the Welsers, he gave them Venezuela. In reality the Spanish crown retained possession of the land but granted the banking family the right to exploit it, if they returned one fifth of the revenue to the crown. These were the usual arrangements the crown made with those who went to the New World, but heretofore, such rights had been reserved exclusively for Spaniards. The Spaniards might hire a foreigner like Columbus, but no foreigners had ever been given the power to establish towns and appoint governors. This Charles gave to the Welsers.

Ambrosius Ehinger, a twenty-nine-year-old relative of several important Welser officials, was appointed first governor of the banking family's domain. So it was that a supposedly stolid, hardheaded German merchant was the first to set off in pursuit of El Dorado.

The scattered Spanish settlements in the New World were alive with tales of golden realms ripe for the taking. The most persistent of these stories was that of *el hombre dorado*, the gilded man. The story happened to be true. It filtered down from the high, almost inaccessible plateau of Cundinamarca, seventy-five hundred feet above sea level in what is now Colombia.

The story was that once a year the king of a land surrounded by mountains covered himself with a sticky substance and then rolled in gold dust. Completely covered, the gilded king walked to the shores of a lake called Guatavita and got into a canoe, paddled out to the center and jumped in to wash off the gold. When he did this, the crowds that had gathered on the shore sent up a great cheer, and this became the signal for the start of a feast.

A nation that could afford to cover its king with gold must have gold in abundance. Such a country would have to rival or surpass Mexico and Peru in wealth. So the thinking went. What no one had bothered to consider is that it does not take that much gold to cover a man's body. Many of the tribes in Central and South America had some gold but not enough to warrant the mounting of an expedition to find it. Only the

Incas and the Aztecs, who had inherited gold collected over a wide area for centuries, had really fabulous quantities.

Ehinger landed at the settlement called Coro on the northern coast of the Welser domain of Venezuela early in 1529. Almost immediately he picked up the rumors of the mountain-dwelling tribe whose king covered himself with gold. According to the stories their land was not far from Coro. The Welsers had not sent Ehinger out to look for gold. His job was to establish the colony on a firm footing and begin exporting profitable products, particularly a substance made from the wood of the guaiac tree which was supposed to cure syphilis. But Ehinger had taken to the life of a conquistador with the enthusiasm of a new convert. Within two months he was off in search of El Dorado, leaving behind only those men who were too ill to travel. He had no idea where he was going, but this did not discourage him in the least. He struck out blindly into the jungle and wandered around for a year. The Welsers assumed he was dead and appointed a new governor, but the new appointee died almost immediately. So, when Ehinger unexpectedly showed up alive, he was able to assume his old position without any trouble.

It took him another year to put together a new expedition, and he was off again. Ehinger still did not know where he was going, but he had developed the theory that if he killed and terrorized enough Indians, they would lead him to the golden land. He cut a swath of devastation through the jungles that the Indians were to remember for generations. The tactics gained him a considerable amount of gold and jewels— nothing like the wealth of the Incas, but a heavy burden nonetheless for an expedition that was struggling through increasingly difficult territory.

Ehinger decided to send a small party back to Coro with

the riches they had collected. A Spaniard named Vascuna, who had been chosen to lead the return party, knew he could not retrace their route because the Indians would be waiting for them and would take vengeance on a small party for what Ehinger had done.

Vascuna and his men tried to find a new route back to Coro but were soon hopelessly lost. Along the way the Indian porters either died or escaped. Each of Vascuna's men was carrying forty pounds of treasure along with his battle gear. It was too much, and the men reluctantly agreed to bury the treasure at the foot of a huge tree. No one has ever been able to locate that tree again.

Even without the burden, the march back to Coro was a nightmare. Dissension broke out and the party split into several smaller groups, making the men tempting prey for the warlike Indians of the region. None of the members of the Vascuna party ever got back to Coro, and only one survived. He was Francisco Martín, who had been taken captive by the Indians and managed to win their confidence. He became a medicine man and thoroughly adopted the ways of his captors.

Meanwhile, Ehinger decided that the Vascuna party had stolen his treasure and abandoned him to die in the jungle, so he struck out again, still in search of the land of gold. His scouts reported that mountains of the type mentioned in the El Dorado legend were nearby. But the transition from steaming lowlands to frigid highlands was too much for the men, already weakened by terrible hardships. Soon, only Ehinger and fifty or so of his strongest men were left out of the hundreds that had started from Coro. Facing a small group rather than an invading army, the attacks of the Indians increased in effectiveness. Finally, in the cold darkness of the mountains near what is now the border of Venezuela and

Colombia, Ehinger abandoned the quest and turned back. Ironically, he was very close to the land in which the legend of El Dorado had originated.

The route back was worse, both for Ehinger's party and for the Indians they encountered. Frustration and failure had increased the terrible German's cruelty. The Indians made desperate attacks in an attempt to stop him. In one of the attacks Ehinger was wounded in the neck. He died three days later. Even without their leader, the survivors managed to destroy several Indian towns. They probably never expected to get out of the jungle alive, and they wouldn't have, had they not luckily encountered Francisco Martín. He interceded with the Indians who had become his friends to allow his countrymen safe passage back to the coast.

Two years and two months after Ehinger had set out on his expedition, a few survivors, with harrowing tales of what they had suffered, returned to Coro. This disaster not only failed to discourage further seekers, it actually whetted their appetites.

Several other expeditions set out in search of the high plateau that held the land of El Dorado. The expeditions were at best unsuccessful and at worst fatal. Then the land in which the El Dorado legend had originated was finally reached, not once but three times by three independent expeditions operating without knowledge of one another.

The first of the three to reach the Cundinamarca plateau, the land of El Dorado, was led by Gonzalo Jiménez de Quesada. Quesada's expedition was launched from the out-of-the-way town of Santa Marta, on the Colombian coast. The colony there was on the verge of ruin and the governor decided the only way to save it was to find the kingdom of El Dorado. He chose Quesada, a lawyer who had turned to more adventurous things, as leader of the expedition. On April 6, 1536, Quesada's well-equipped expedition set off westward from Santa Marta. Included in the party were 620 foot soldiers and 85 horsemen. Two brigantines were used to carry the bulk of the expedition's baggage up navigable rivers.

Quesada is perhaps the most admirable of all the leaders of El Dorado searches. In general, he preferred to remain at peace with the Indians and to gain their cooperation through friendship rather than terror. But the expedition ran into bad luck almost at once. They entered territory Ehinger had slashed through years before, and the Indians were not inclined to be friendly. They found other relics of the Ehinger disaster—some Spaniards who had deserted from Ehinger. They offered to guide the new seekers. Foolishly Quesada accepted, and the new guides quickly got everyone lost. It was weeks before the expedition managed to work its way back to the river upon which they hoped to find the long overdue brigantines with fresh supplies. The ships had suffered the usual disasters along the way but finally did arrive with enough food and other supplies to allow Quesada to lead his men even farther into the treacherous swampland.

Years later a survivor of the Quesada expedition set down this description: "Quesada saw his numerous troops diminished by fevers and sores from the plagues of travel, ticks, bats, mosquitoes, serpents, crocodiles, tigers (jaguars), hunger, calamities and miseries with other ills which pass description . . . breaking through thickest woods and bridging the swamps and creeks, consuming the whole torrid days in incredible labors so that with innumerable ink the fifth part could not be told."

Food was a major problem. Usually such expeditions obtained food by trade or plunder from Indian villages. But

Quesada was still passing through land visited by Ehinger. The terror he had spread was so great that six years later the land remained virtually uninhabited, and Quesada's men were reduced to boiling their leather scabbards and eating them.

Ultimately, however, Quesada reached the mountains where Ehinger had stopped. He now had 166 men remaining under his command—the rest had either died along the way or returned to Santa Marta on the brigantines. Quesada gained the confidence of an Indian chief who led them to a pass through the mountains that had defeated Ehinger. They had entered the land of El Dorado. It was the plateau of Cundinamarca "the land of the condor."

The land itself was far from the golden kingdom built by the inflamed imaginations of the seekers. The Cundinamarca plateau was inhabited by a people called Chibachas. Culturally the Chibachas were superior to the rather primitive tribesmen of the surrounding lowlands, but there was no possible comparison between the Chibachas and the Incas or Aztecs.

Worst of all, from the viewpoint of the Dorado seekers, the plateau of Cundinamarca contained no gold. The Chibachas themselves possessed a limited number of golden ornaments, but they had obtained the gold by trading their chief product, salt, with lowlanders who mined the metal.

The plateau was a disappointment, but there is no doubt that here was the origin of the El Dorado legend. It was a Chibachas chief who covered himself with gold dust and plunged into Lake Guatavita to the cheers of the multitude. Unfortunately, the ceremony itself had been abandoned some forty years before the coming of Quesada, presumably because it was a waste of scarce gold.

But the dorado rite apparently had been a spectacle to be remembered for its fame spread to the lowland tribes and outward to the coastal cities where the Spanish planted their outposts. The mystery and grandeur of the story was enhanced because the Chibachas lived in a place very difficult to reach.

Quesada reached the land of the Chibachas in January of 1537 and spent almost two years subduing it. Although he seems to have acted with unusual kindness and tolerance for a conquistador, the results were the same. The Chibacha state was destroyed and everything the people had was stolen.

At first it seemed to Quesada's men that they had indeed discovered the El Dorado of their dreams. But they soon learned that all the gold of the natives of Cundinamarca was on display; there were no storehouses and no mines. The best single haul the Spaniards could make was some two hundred pounds of pure gold obtained after the capture of one of the major Indian cities. They scoured the plateau from one end to the other looking for the hidden treasure houses of gold they were sure existed somewhere. Only slowly and grudgingly did it dawn on Quesada and his men that they had not found a new Peru. Still, they consoled themselves they had conquered new territory and they had obtained some treasure.

At the beginning of 1539 Quesada was thinking about returning to Santa Marta, when he received some disconcerting news: a large, splendidly equipped party of Spaniards was preparing to ascend the plateau of Cundinamarca.

Leader of the new party was the magnificent, dashing, brilliant and unscrupulous Sebastián de Belalcázar, one of the men who had been with Pizarro during the conquest of Peru. The conquest had made Belalcázar rich, and Pizarro had granted him nominal control over the northernmost portions of the old Inca realm, in what is now Ecuador. Belalcázar roamed his new domain looking for gold and not finding nearly as much as he wanted.

All previous attempts to reach the land of El Dorado had been made from the north. But the route from Cundinamarca south was much easier. Many natives from the plateau traveled southward. In 1535 one of them reached the city of Quinto where Belalcázar was governing virtually like a king, much to the irritation of Pizarro. This native apparently gave Belalcázar a firsthand account of the ceremony of the gilded man but omitted the detail that it was no longer being performed. Belalcázar himself may have coined the phrase "El Dorado," and given the story its final polish.

Belalcázar was told that the land of El Dorado lay a mere twelve days' journey from Quinto. But when he set out from Quinto in 1536 he led an enormous force provisioned for a march that might last for years. In this Belalcázar had been foresighted. His journey was by far the easiest of all the dorado seekers, but he traveled slowly, conquering as he went. At the beginning of 1539 Belalcázar got close enough to the plateau upon which the land of El Dorado lay to hear that another group of Spaniards had already conquered the land.

Quesada had sent his brother Hernán Pérez to meet Belalcázar's party, and as he was nervously awaiting Hernán Pérez's return, he received an even more disconcerting piece of news. Yet another group of Spaniards was advancing on the land of El Dorado.

This information was not completely correct. The leader of the third group was not a Spaniard but a German, Nikolaus Federmann, another of the Welser men. The Welsers had a run of unusually bad luck in picking men to send to Venezuela. Ehinger had become obsessed searching for El Dorado. Federmann was a young German knight, loosely attached to the Welser interests, who had come to the New World for adventure. During one of Ehinger's absenses from Coro, Federmann was appointed temporary governor. Instead of looking after the Welser interests he immediately set out on his own six-month quest for El Dorado. He did not find the golden land that time, but he came away with the conviction that he was the man destined to find El Dorado. After Ehinger died in the jungle, Federmann thought he would get the governorship, but he didn't. In 1534 Georg Hohemut landed at Coro with credentials indicating that he was Ehinger's successor. And he proved to be a worthy successor for within a year Hohemut was organizing his own El Dorado expedition. Hohemut's wanderings lasted three years and two weeks, covered fifteen hundred miles, and reached (in a very round-about way) the mountains shielding the plateau of Cundinamarca. But, like Ehinger, Hohemut was not able to find a way up to the plateau, so, discouraged and broken in health, he returned to Coro, only to find that Federmann had long since departed to look for El Dorado again. In fact, Federmann had set off almost immediately after Hohemut, and he wandered longer, but at least he found the land.

Of the three parties that met on the plateau of Cundinamarca in February 1539, Federmann's was the most tattered. Federmann was well acquainted with the history of the dorado legends. He knew, or should have known, that if the land of the gilded man was anywhere it lay in the mountains to the west of Coro. Yet he headed in a southeasterly direction. His probable reason was that he was taking great pains to avoid Hohemut, who was also heading toward the mountains. For Federmann to strike out on his own was an act of gross insubordination. To keep from running into his erstwhile chief, Federmann unfortunately wandered into the grassy plains of the Orinoco River basin. These plains called *llanos* are a hot, trackless mass of marshes and high grass. Federmann and his men wandered around in them for a year, before finally striking westward again. It took another year to reach the mountain chain, and a third year before a pass through the mountains into the land of El Dorado could be found. And when he got there he found the land was full of Spaniards.

An improbable meeting of the three seekers of the gilded man took place in February 1539. They had all reached the land of their dreams and found that it fell far short of expectations. Since the plateau of Cundinamarca was hardly worth fighting about, the three got on excellently. Quesada gave Federmann, who had nothing, a share of the gold he had found. Belalcázar didn't need any handouts. He was satisfied with the territories he had conquered on his way to the land of El Dorado. Both latecomers agreed to recognize Quesada's prior claim to the plateau, and after a few pleasant months the three returned to the coast and sailed together to Europe to petition Charles V to parcel out the land they had discovered in their separate quests.

Federmann again hoped he would be appointed governor of Venezuela. (Hohemut, worn out by his quest, had died.) But the Welsers were not anxious to put their trust in a man who so impetuously abandoned his duty to search for phantom lands of gold. They appointed someone else. (The man they appointed, Philipp von Hutten, also went seeking El Dorado. His neglect of the Welsers' Venezuela interests led to a revolt in which von Hutten lost his life when he returned from his search, and ultimately led to the revocation of the Welsers' South American grant.) After this disappointment Federmann never returned to South America. He wrote up his travels, and as far as we know that was the last noteworthy thing he did in his life.

Belalcázar was more favorably received in Europe. He was given a governorship and in 1541 returned to South America, where he quickly became involved in the bloody power struggles that racked Pizarro's Peru. He managed to come out of them alive, but then became ill and died while still quite young.

Quesada was destined to become the Don Quixote of the El Dorado story. He fared poorly at Charles' court. His enemies outmaneuvered him and robbed him of the spoils of his conquest. Ultimately he returned to South America, where for years he lived a life of honorable poverty and continued to dream of gold. Although Gonzalo Jiménez de Quesada had really discovered the land of El Dorado, he refused to believe it.

When Quesada went to Spain, he left his younger brother Hernán Pérez in charge of the plateau of Cundinamarca. Hernán dredged the lake of the dorado ceremony and found some gold, but not nearly as much as he thought there would be. So he convinced himself that this was not really the land of El Dorado after all, and he began looking around for another place where there was a lake surrounded by mountains in which a gilded king washed himself. He decided the golden realm lay to the east. Somehow he overlooked or ignored the the fact that Federmann had spent years wandering in that very region and had encountered nothing but the *llanos*. Hernán Pérez was not able to launch an extensive expedition of his own, but many began to share his illusion that El Dorado was still undiscovered.

In Peru to the south, another younger brother of another famous man was busily weaving fantasies about the splendors of an El Dorado to the east. This was Gonzalo Pizarro, youngest brother of the conqueror of the Incas. By 1543 the El Dorado legend had grown enormously. The chronicler of Gonzalo Pizarro's expedition sets down these reasons for the quest:

"He [Gonzalo] decided to go and search . . . for a great monarch who is called El Dorado (concerning whose wealth there are many rumors in these parts). Upon being questioned by me as to the reason why they call that monarch Chief El Dorado or King El Dorado, the Spaniards who have been in Quinto . . . say that what has been gathered from the Indians is that the great lord or monarch constantly goes about covered with gold ground into dust and as fine as ground salt; for it is his opinion that to wear any other adornment is less beautifying, and that to put on pieces or a coat of arms hammered out of gold or stamped out or fabricated in any other way is a sign of vulgarity and a common thing, and that other rich lords and monarchs wear such things when it pleases them to do so; but to powder one's self with gold is an extraordinary thing to do, unusual and new and more costly, inasmuch as what one puts on in the morning every day is removed and washed off in the evening and is cast away and thrown to waste on the ground; and this he does every day of his life."

Gonzalo Pizarro's well-equipped, well-financed expedition set out early in 1541 and rapidly turned into a major disaster. Gonzalo inflicted hideous tortures on the local Indians in the belief that they would direct him to the realm of El Dorado. Of course the Indians knew nothing and so could tell him nothing. Finally some of the Indians decided that the only possible way to get rid of the madman was to satisfy him with stories that the gold lay somewhere close by, but not so close that he could easily return when he did not find it.

The Gonzalo Pizarro expedition wandered aimlessly and hopelessly around the jungles for nearly two years, finding nothing. But one of the offshoots of the expedition found the land of the famed warrior women, the Amazons—or did they find it? Here is what happened. At one point conditions had become so desperate that Pizarro's men built some brigantines to sail downriver to search for food for the men. The brigantines, commanded by Francisco de Orellana, a relative of the Pizarro family, just kept right on sailing until they reached safety at the coast. Whether Orellana had simply abandoned Gonzalo or was prevented from returning by his men is a point that is still debated today. Whatever the reason, Orellana's foraging trip turned into one of the most remarkable inland voyages ever made. In poorly constructed brigantines he navigated the entire length of the world's mightiest river, the river that was to be named Amazon.

The legend of the Amazons, the warrior women, is an ancient one going all the way back to the Greeks. The word Amazon apparently comes from a Greek phrase meaning "without breast," a description taken from the Amazon's custom of amputating the right breast so that they could draw a bow without interference.

From ancient times right up to the time of the conquest of the New World, the kingdom of the Amazons has been sought in many places. And when the New World was found, some believed that this lost kingdom must certainly be somewhere in the new lands. The Spaniards themselves were great readers of romantic novels and one of the most popular of the time concerned discovery of a kingdom of women in Mexico. Many took this romance as fact, and the stories of the Amazons multiplied.

Father Gaspar de Carvajal took part in Orellana's extraordinary odyssey and wrote an account of it. His reliability as a reporter has often been questioned, particularly because of his description of an encounter with the Amazons:

"These women are very white and tall, and have hair very long and braided and wound about the head, and they are very robust and go about naked, with their privy parts covered, with their bows and arrows in their hand, doing as much fighting as ten Indian men, and indeed there was one woman among these who shot an arrow a span deep into one of the brigantines, and others less deep, so that our brigantines looked like porcupines."

The Spaniards claimed only to have seen a few of the Amazons, during a brief fight along the river, but the stories they got from all the natives indicated that some sort of kingdom ruled by women existed in the area. Today many anthropologists believe that neither the Indians nor the Spanish were necessarily fabricating the stories of the Amazons, for they still persist among tribes along the river. It is possible that a matriarchic warrior society may once have existed in the Amazon jungle and that the natives retained stories of it. Some even believe that the remnants of a true Amazon society may still exist in some inaccessible regions near the river.

While Orellana was being whisked downstream on his great and unintentional voyage of discovery, he heard that somewhere to the north lay the golden kingdom ruled by a people called the Omaguas. This fixed the location of El Dorado more firmly as being in the area of Guiana, a region that had remained unexplored. Shortly the area was to become crowded with seekers, because yet another story became attached to it. This concerned a band of fugitive Incas from Peru who fled to Guiana with a horde of treasure that Pizarro had missed.

The fact that much exploring had already been conducted, without the slightest success, coupled with the ghastly examples of the fate of most dorado seekers, discouraged no one. There were always more hints. Philipp von Hutten, last of the German dorado seekers, had actually reached the outskirts of some of the Omagua villages but had been driven off by ferocious resistance. Ultimately it turned out that the Omaguas were not a particularly rich or advanced people, but von Hutten's men had only a glimpse of the Omagua realm. To their imaginations, it seemed as though they had almost reached the realm of gold. At least that is what the tale sounded like after it reached the coast of South America and had been transmitted to Spain.

At first El Dorado expeditions were few, and were undertaken by only the most daring, but by the middle of the sixteenth century they had become almost commonplace. Every Spaniard with enough money to equip an expedition was trying frantically to obtain royal permission to find El Dorado. At one point a governmental oversight placed two expeditions in the same spot at the same time. The result was a battle in which both expeditions were virtually exterminated.

Living in quiet dissatisfaction at Bogotá was Gonzalo Jiménez de Quesada. While others had their eyes fixed on Guiana, Quesada had, for some unknown reason, remained convinced that the kingdom was located in the brutal *llanos* country which stretched out from the foothills of the Andes. What makes Quesada's obsession particularly odd is that he knew perfectly well that Federmann had wandered all through the *llanos*. Other seekers, including Quesada's own younger brother had also combed the *llanos*, without finding a trace of El Dorado.

Quesada repeatedly petitioned the king of Spain for permission to explore the land, and after years of frustrating delay, the permission was granted. In his years of living as a private citizen, Quesada had retained the reputation as a hero that he had won with his conquest of Cundinamarca. There was no difficulty finding men to serve under such a commander. Quesada's second great expedition set out in 1569, thirty years after the meeting of the three dorado seekers in the land of El Dorado. Quesada was close to seventy years old and he led an army of four hundred armed Spaniards and hundreds of Indian bearers off in search of his old dream.

The climate of the *llanos* had not improved in the thirty years since it had reduced Nikolaus Federmann's expedition to a half-naked group of starving and desperate men. After a three-year journey of unusually frightful hardships, twenty-five ragged Spaniards, four Indians and a few bony horses limped back to Bogotá. Leading them was the indomitable Quesada, now around seventy-three. He had outlived most of the younger men of his expedition.

Even after this disaster he did not consider the possibility that he might have been wrong. No, he had simply taken the wrong path, but next time . . . and he went ahead planning a new quest. By this time Quesada was, without a doubt, absolutely insane on the subject of El Dorado. But few regarded him that way. They listened with respect to the old man's schemes. When Bogotá was threatened by an Indian uprising in 1575, the citizens chose Gonzalo Jiménez de Quesada to command their army, even though he was too old and feeble to ride a horse and had to be carried to the scene of the battle in a hammock. But Quesada planned a winning campaign, and as the end of the battle neared he somehow found the strength to mount his horse and lead the final charge with lance in hand. He lived another four years, dying quietly when nearly eighty.

Quesada lends a note of nobility to the generally sordid story of the El Dorado questers. He had made nothing from his searches and died a poor man. The only thing he could leave was his royal grant to search for El Dorado. Quesada had never married and did not even have any illegitimate children. His closest living relative was a niece in Spain. She had married a successful middle-aged professional soldier, Antonio de Berrio, and so to Berrio fell old Quesada's grant to search for the golden kingdom. Along with it Berrio seemed also to inherit the old man's obsession, because next to Quesada himself, Antonio de Berrio was to become the most persistent seeker of El Dorado.

Between 1580, when he first sailed for the New World, and 1595, Berrio was a whirlwind of activity. He studied the records of all the previous doradists and decided that the land of the gilded man lay not in the *llanos* as Quesada had thought, but in Guiana. He led three remarkable expeditions through this largely unexplored territory, set up towns and trading posts and managed to quarrel with just about every Spaniard who had any power in the region. The quarrels were not necessarily Berrio's fault. His belief in El Dorado was so firm and his energy so great that others thought he really was going to discover the gold, and they were trying to head him off so they could get it for themselves.

But by 1595 South America, which had long been almost exclusively a Spanish enterprise, was becoming increasingly interesting to the rest of the world, most notably the English. The English were looking for ways of deflecting the Spanish gold flow to their own country. One of the most effective ways was piracy. So on April 8, 1595, Berrio and a group of

Spaniards were captured by a roving English adventurer. He was Sir Walter Raleigh. Berrio was a great explorer, but he is best remembered for infecting Raleigh with a severe and ultimately fatal case of El Dorado plague.

Of course Raleigh was extremely susceptible. He already had a great interest in the New World, and a few years earlier his scheme to establish a colony in Virginia had ended in failure. Raleigh's greatest asset had been the personal favor of Queen Elizabeth, but because of his extravagant ambitions he made too many enemies and the Queen was no longer kindly disposed. Still, in 1595 she granted him the right to raise a small fleet and sail to the New World to harass the Spanish and to search for the kingdom of El Dorado. Raleigh was well acquainted with all the dorado stories and like Berrio had become convinced that the kingdom lay in the Guiana area.

This kingdom now had a name besides El Dorado. It was called Manoa and was located on a great lake called Parima. The names came from a survivor of one of the previous El Dorado disasters who had been captured by the Indians, lived among them ten years and finally emerged from the jungle with wild and wonderful tales of the land of gold in Guiana.

Raleigh collected all the tales and wrote down the final and most spectacular version of the El Dorado story: ". . . when the Emperor [of the Guianians] carouseth with his captains, tributories and governors, the manner is thus. All those that pledge him are first stripped naked, and their bodies anointed all over with a kind of white balsam . . . when they are anointed all over, certain servants of the Emperor having prepared gold made into fine powder blow it through hollow canes upon their naked bodies, until they be all shining from the foot to the head, and in this sort they sit drinking by twenties and hundreds and continue in drunknness sometimes six or seven days together . . ."

In 1595 Raleigh captured Berrio but was not able really to penetrate Guiana. He returned to England more firmly convinced than ever that he could find the kingdom ruled by the golden monarch. He did not envision a mere conquest of El Dorado but drew up elaborate plans for establishing an equitable relationship between Guiana and England. It was the sort of thing the Spanish never considered.

Raleigh's fortunes suffered even a more severe decline after 1595, and twenty years elapsed before he could return to the New World. Much of that time he spent locked in the Tower of London, under sentence of death on a trumped-up charge of treason.

In 1616 Raleigh was released from prison and allowed to raise a fleet to sail to Guiana. King James I, the reigning monarch, had not forgiven Raleigh, or even lifted the death sentence which hung over him. He just suspended it until such time as he saw what Raleigh could bring back from Guiana. It was a strange act for a king who never seems to have been dazzled by dreams of golden lands. It was doubly strange because James was working hard to establish good relations with Spain, and here he was allowing Raleigh to sail right into the Spanish domain. Raleigh was made to promise he would not invade any Spanish territory, an impossible promise, since all the territory was claimed by Spain.

Perhaps if Raleigh had really found El Dorado all his transgressions would have been forgiven. But he did not find it because there was none, and, worse, he made a complete mess of his expedition. Not only did he invade Spanish territory but some of his men foolishly stormed a Spanish town and killed the governor. Raleigh's own favorite son died in the attack. In the end some of Raleigh's men stole ships and sailed off to become pirates plundering Spanish possessions.

King James was furious and even offered to allow the Spaniards to execute the hated Raleigh themselves if they wished, but the English public would never have stood for that, for through it all Raleigh remained a hero of sorts. If he had to die, it would be on his native soil. The execution took place at Westminster. All the chronicles of the time indicate it was a grand spectacle, and Raleigh died gallantly. The dream of El Dorado died with him—not all at once, but the great days of questing were, for all practical purposes, over.

As late as the eighteenth century European mapmakers kept including Manoa and Lake Parima on their maps. A few small expeditions set out to look for them, but enthusiasm had definitely waned.

Since the search for El Dorado had started with a German, perhaps it was fitting that it end with one. The man who finally put the lid on the whole El Dorado business was that energetic Prussian natural scientist and traveler Alexander von Humboldt. At the beginning of the nineteenth century Humboldt conducted an extensive reconnaissance of South America. He retraced the routes of most of the dorado seekers and concluded that not only was there no Manoa, there was not even a Lake Parima in the interior of Guiana. He did find a river Parima, which in time of flood may have looked like a lake and given rise to the legend. But there was not a trace of the golden kingdom. Faced with so formidable and overwhelming a testimony, the land of El Dorado was banished from the world's maps.

BIBLIOGRAPHY

A complete bibliography seems unnecessary in a general book of this type. What follows is a selected list of books the reader may find interesting and readily available.

Arciniegas, Germán. *Germans in the Conquest of America*. New York: The Macmillan Co., 1943.
Ashe, Geoffrey. *King Arthur's Avalon*. New York: E. P. Dutton & Co., 1955.
——*Land to the West*. New York: The Viking Press, 1962.
Atkinson, R. J. C. *Stonehenge*. New York: The Macmillan Co., 1956.
——*Stonehenge and Avebury*. London: Her Majesty's Stationery Office, 1959.
Bacon, Edward (editor). *Vanished Civilizations of the Ancient World*. New York: McGraw-Hill Co., 1963.
Bellamy, H. S. *The Atlantis Myth*. London: Faber and Faber, 1936.
Bibby, Geoffrey. *Four Thousand Years Ago*. New York: Alfred A. Knopf, 1962.
——*The Testimony of the Spade*. New York: Alfred A. Knopf, 1956.
Blavatsky, Helena Petrovna. *The Secret Doctrine*. Adyar India: Theosophical Publishing House.
Bolland, Charles Michael. *They All Discovered America*. New York: Doubleday & Co., Inc., 1961.

Bullfinch, Thomas. *The Age of Chivalry*, edited by E. E. Hale. Boston: Lothrop, Lee & Shepard Co., 1884.

Burland, C. A. *The Gods of Mexico*. New York: G. P. Putnam's Sons, 1967.

Carrington, Richard. *A Guide to Earth History*. London: Chatto & Windus, 1956.

Caton-Thompson, Gertrude. *The Zimbabwe Culture*. Oxford: Clarendon Press, 1931.

Cayce, Edgar Evans. *Edgar Cayce on Atlantis*. New York: Paperback Library, Inc., 1968.

Ceram, C. W. *Gods, Graves and Scholars* (revised edition). New York: Alfred A. Knopf, Inc., 1967.

——(editor). *Hands on the Past*. New York: Alfred A. Knopf, Inc., 1967.

Chambers, Erik. *Arthur of Britain*. London: Cambridge Speculum Historiale, 1964.

Chapman, Walker. *The Golden Dream*. New York: Bobbs-Merrill Co., Inc., 1967.

——*The Search for El Dorado*. New York: Bobbs-Merrill Co., Inc., 1967.

Churchward, James. *The Children of Mu*. New York: Paperback Library, Inc., 1968.

——*The Lost Continent of Mu*. New York: Paperback Library, Inc., 1968.

——*The Sacred Symbols of Mu*. New York: Paperback Library, Inc., 1968.

Coe, Michael D. *Mexico*. New York: Frederick Praeger, 1962.

Cohen, Daniel. *Myths of the Space Age*. New York: Dodd, Mead & Co., 1967.

Cottrell, Leonard. *The Horizon Book of Lost Worlds*. New York: American Heritage Publishing Co., Inc., 1962.

——*Seeing Roman Britain*. London: Pan Books, Ltd., 1967.

Crampton, Patrick. *Stonehenge of the Kings*. New York: John Day Co., Inc., 1968.

Daniel, Glyn. *Man Discovers His Past*. New York: Thomas Y. Crowell, Co., 1968.

——*The Megalith Builders of Western Europe*. London: Penguin Books, 1968.

Davidson, Basil. *The African Past*. Boston: Little, Brown and Co., 1964.

——*The Lost Cities of Africa*. Boston: Little, Brown and Co., 1959.

De Camp, L. Sprague. *The Ancient Engineers*. New York: Doubleday & Co., Inc., 1963.

——and De Camp, Catherine. *Ancient Ruins and Archaeology*. New York: Doubleday & Co., Inc., 1964.

———and Ley, Willy. *Lands Beyond.* New York: Rinehart & Co., 1952.

———*Lost Continents.* New York: The Gnome Press, 1954.

———and De Camp, Catherine. *Spirits, Stars and Spells.* New York: Canaveral Press, 1966.

Deuel, Leo (editor). *Conquistadors Without Swords.* New York: St. Martin's Press, Inc., 1967.

———*Testaments of Time.* New York: Alfred A. Knopf, 1965.

———(editor) *Treasures of Time.* New York: Avon Books, 1964.

Diaz del Castillo, Bernal. *The Discovery and Conquest of Mexico.* New York: Farrar, Straus and Cudahy, 1956.

Donnelly, Ignatius. *Atlantis: The Antediluvian World.* Many editions, 1882–1967.

Geoffrey of Monmouth. *History of the Kings of Britain.* New York: E. P. Dutton & Co., 1958.

Hall, R. N. *Great Zimbabwe, Mashonaland and Rhodesia.* London: Methuen & Co., 1925.

Hapgood, Charles H. *Maps of the Ancient Sea Kings.* Philadelphia: Chilton Books, 1965.

Hawkes, Jacquetta. *Early Britain.* London: William Collins, 1955.

———*A Land.* New York: Random House, Inc., 1951.

———(editor). *The World of the Past* (2 vols.). New York: Alfred A. Knopf, 1963.

Hawkins, Gerald S. *Stonehenge Decoded.* New York: Doubleday & Co., Inc., 1965.

Herrmann, Paul. *Conquest by Man.* New York: Harper and Brothers, 1954.

———*The Great Age of Discovery.* New York: Harper and Brothers, 1958.

Heyerdahl, Thor. *Aku-Aku.* New York: Rand McNally & Co., 1958.

———*American Indians in the Pacific.* New York: Rand McNally & Co., 1950.

———*Kon Tiki.* New York: Rand McNally & Co., 1950.

Hope-Moncrieff, A. R. *Romance and Legend of Chivalry.* New York: William H. Wise and Co., 1934.

Le Plongeon, Augustus. *Queen Moo and the Egyptian Sphinx.* London: Keyan, Paul, Trench, Trubner and Co., 1896.

McNeill, William H. *The Rise of the West.* Chicago: The University of Chicago Press, 1963.

———*A World History.* New York: Oxford University Press, 1967.

Malory, Sir Thomas. *The Works of Sir Thomas Malory.* London: Oxford University Press, 1954.

Mandeville, Sir John. *The Travels of Sir John Mandeville with Three Narratives in Illustration of It: The Voyage of Johannes de Plao Carpini, The Journal of Friar William de Rubruquis, The*

Journal of Friar Odoric, edited by A. W. Pollard. New York: Dover Publications, Inc., 1964.

Metraux, Alfred. *Easter Island, A Stone-Age Civilization of the Pacific*. New York: Oxford University Press, 1957.

Moorehead, Alan. *The Fatal Impact*. New York: Harper and Row Publishers, 1966.

Newall, R. S. *Stonehenge*. London: Her Majesty's Stationery Office, 1959.

Oldenbourg, Zoe. *The Crusades*. New York: Random House, Inc., 1966.

Piggott, Stuart. *Prehistoric India*. London: Penguin Books, 1950.

Pohl, Frederick. *Atlantic Crossings Before Columbus*. New York: W. W. Norton and Co., Inc., 1961.

Prescott, William H. *History of the Conquest of Mexico* (3 vols.). Philadelphia: J. B. Lippincott and Co., 1875.

Previte-Orton, C. W. *The Shorter Cambridge Medieval History* (2 vols.). Cambridge: The University Press, 1952.

Radford, C. A. Ralegh. *The Pictorial History of Glastonbery Abbey, The Isle of Avalon*. London: Pitkin Pictorials Ltd., 1966.

Rapport, Samuel and Wright, Helen (editors). *Archaeology*. New York: Washington Square Press, Inc., 1964.

Reed, Alma M. *The Ancient Past of Mexico*. New York: Crown Publishers, Inc., 1966.

Robbins, Roland Wells and Jones, Even. *Hidden America*. New York: Alfred A. Knopf, 1959.

Schreiber, Hermann and Georg. *Vanished Cities*. New York: Alfred A. Knopf, 1957.

Silverberg, Robert. *Frontiers in Archaeology*. Philadelphia: Chilton Books, 1966.

———*Empires in the Dust*. Philadelphia: Chilton Books, 1963.

———*Lost Cities and Vanished Civilizations*. Philadelphia: Chilton Books, 1962.

———*Mound Builders of Ancient America*. Greenwich, Conn.: New York Graphic Society, Ltd., 1968.

———*Scientists and Scoundrels*. New York: Thomas Y. Crowell Co., 1965.

Simpson, George Gaylord. *The Geography of Evolution*. New York: Capricorn Books, 1965.

Skelton, R. A., Marston Thomas G., and Painter, George O. *The Vinland Map and the Tartar Relation*. New Haven: Yale University Press, 1965.

Slessarev, Vesevold. *Prester John: The Letter and the Legend*. Minneapolis: The University of Minnesota Press, 1959.

Spence, Lewis. *Atlantis in America*. New York: Brentano's, 1925.

——*Encyclopedia of Occultism*. New York: University Books, Inc., 1960.

——*The Problem of Atlantis*. New York: Brentano's, 1925.

——*The Problem of Lemuria*. Philadelphia: David McKay Company, 1933.

Stacy-Judd, Robert B. *Atlantis-Mother of Empires*. Los Angeles: DeVorss and Co., 1939.

Stearn, Jess. *Edgar Cayce: The Sleeping Prophet*. New York: Doubleday & Co., Inc., 1967.

Suggs, Robert C. *Lords of the Blue Pacific*. Greenwich, Conn.: New York Graphic Society, Ltd., 1962.

Wendt, Herbert. *It Began in Babel*. Boston: Houghton Mifflin Co., 1962.

Wheeler, Sir Mortimer. *Archaeology From the Earth*. Baltimore: Penguin Books, 1954.

——*Civilizations of the Indus Valley and Beyond*. New York: McGraw-Hill Book Co., 1966.

Zahm, J. A. *The Quest of El Dorado*. New York: D. Appleton and Co., 1917.

INDEX